THE DIARIES OF
Sir Daniel Gooch

THE DIARIES OF
Sir Daniel Gooch

INTRODUCTION BY
SIR THEODORE MARTIN

NONSUCH

First published 1892
Copyright © in this edition 2006
Nonsuch Publishing Ltd

Nonsuch Publishing Limited
The Mill, Brimscombe Port, Stroud, Gloucestershire, GL5 2QG
www.nonsuch-publishing.com

Nonsuch Publishing Ltd is an imprint of the Tempus Publishing Group

British Library Cataloguing in Publication Data.
A catalogue record for this book is available from the British Library.

ISBN 1-84588-016-1

Typesetting and origination by Nonsuch Publishing Limited
Printed in Great Britain by Oaklands Book Services Limited

CONTENTS

INTRODUCTION TO THE MODERN EDITION

It was perhaps inevitable that Daniel Gooch (1816–1889) would become a great railway engineer. When he was a boy, George Stephenson, father of the the steam railway, builder of the famous *Rocket* locomotive and a friend of his father, would take the young Gooch on his knee and talk to him about engineering. At the age of ten or twelve his father bought him a lathe and a box of tools and at fifteen he got a job at the Tredegar Ironworks in Monmouthshire, where his father also worked. His time there he regarded as 'by far the best school for a young engineer'; he later worked at the world's first railway locomotive-building company, run by George Stephenson's son, Robert, in Newcastle-upon-Tyne. He joined the Great Western Railway as Locomotive Superintendent when he was just twenty-one years old, and would remain associated with the company for most of the rest of his life.

The GWR had been founded in 1833, largely to ensure that the port of Bristol remained a viable alternative to Liverpool. Isambard Kingdom Brunel was appointed chief engineer and decided to lay broad-gauge track, despite the fact that all the other railway companies used the much narrower standard-gauge, which would necessitate passengers changing trains where the two gauges met. Brunel's rationale was that the broad-gauge would allow trains to travel more quickly than on standard-gauge track, and the locomotives designed and built for the broad-gauge track under the superintendence of Daniel Gooch (340 over twenty-seven years) were faster and safer than anything that had gone before. During the 1840s and 1850s the railway companies competed in the 'Gauge War' as the GWR expanded its routes, but by the 1860s it was accepted that the days of broad-gauge track were numbered, although it took until 1892 for it to disappear entirely.

Daniel Gooch resigned from the company in 1864 to concentrate on laying the first underwater telegraph cable across the Atlantic Ocean. Three attempts had already been made in 1857 and 1858, but had ended in failure. In 1864 Gooch became chairman of the Telegraph Construction & Maintenance Company and chartered the *Great Eastern*, the vast steam-ship that had been Brunel's final project, to lay the cable. Their first attempt, in 1865, was also unsuccessful, the cable breaking after 1,000 miles had been paid out, but, the following year, a telegraph cable was finally laid across the Atlantic, covering a distance of approximately 1,750 miles.

Gooch was asked to return to the GWR in 1865, this time as chairman. The company was in financial difficulties but, under Gooch's chairmanship, it returned to profitability and he remained at the head of the company until his death. As well as the transition from broad-gauge to standard-gauge track, he oversaw the construction of the Severn Tunnel. At the time, this was the longest underwater tunnel in the world, took thirteen years to build and is still in use today. This, together with the success of the GWR and the revolution in communications brought about by the transatlantic telegraph cable, constitutes the legacy of Daniel Gooch, one of the greatest engineers of the nineteenth century.

INTRODUCTORY NOTICE

Sir Daniel Gooch left voluminous diaries; and it was his wish that extracts from these, either illustrative of his career, or bearing upon the works of national importance with which he was connected, should be made public. By industry, steady perseverance, and the influence of a character which inspired confidence in all with whom he was brought into contact, he had become, like Horace, "ex humili potens," and, like Horace, he was justifiably proud of the fact. He had many friends, who, he naturally thought, might feel interest in the story of his life; but perhaps his strongest reason for desiring to tell it was, that it might operate as a guiding light and incentive to the many who live by labour, to thousands of whom he was personally known, and the welfare of whose class was always present to his thoughts as an object to be steadily pursued.

From his boyhood, happy in the training of a home in which parental discipline was tempered by affection, and "pure religion teaching household laws" prevailed, he seems early to have determined that, if he did not make a career for himself, it should not be for want of application and self-control. The wise counsel of his mother, that he should

keep pressing onward and upward, fell upon no heedless
ear. It was his rule through life. It led him to seize every
opportunity of acquiring the knowledge for which his
natural genius gave him a bias. However scanty his earnings,
he lived within them, that he might be free from the
distractions and the slavery of debt. Always to turn out work
the best he could make it, and to make his employers feel
that this completeness, far more than the question of wages,
was uppermost in his mind, brought its natural reward in
the regard it inspired, and in procuring for him such early
opportunities for advancement as could have been gained
in no other way. Hard, honest, conscientious work, a quick
eye to see where improvements were wanted and might be
made, and the patience and perseverance required for their
accomplishment,—these were the basis of his success in life
in a field where he had many men of great ability for his
competitors.

The name of Sir Daniel Gooch is inseparably connected
with the establishment and growth of railways and of ocean
telegraphic communication. While yet only twenty-one
years old, he was appointed, on the recommendation of Mr.
Brunel, to superintend the locomotive department of the
Great Western Railway, then in the course of construction,
and he very soon showed that, young as he was, he had
shot ahead of the locomotive engine-makers of the time
by the construction of engines of greater power and more
economical in working than any which, up to that date, they
had been able to turn out. Like the Great Western engineer,
Mr. Brunel, he was an enthusiastic advocate of the broad
gauge, and fought for it in the front rank of the Battle of
the Gauges—a conflict of now merely historical interest, but
carried on for years with a fury of which only those who
were partakers in it could form an idea. To the last Sir Daniel

adhered to his conviction, that the broad gauge would have been the best and cheapest for the country. But he admitted that the preponderance of the narrow gauge, which, for the lighter loads that prevail through the minor ramifications of the railway system is assuredly the more appropriate, made the ultimate abandonment of the broad gauge inevitable; and before his death he was preparing the way for that abandonment, which is now being carried out. In his diary he alludes with justice to the gain which the country reaped from this conflict of the gauges, putting on their mettle, as it did, the engineering giants by whom the conflict was carried on, and leading through their rivalry to improvements in speed, economy, and comfort which might otherwise have been long postponed.

Soon after Sir Daniel's appointment to the Great Western Railway Company, he was instructed by the Board to provide drawings for the engines wanted to meet the growth of the traffic. The engines built upon his designs, unlike those by other makers with which he had to work on the opening of the earlier sections of the railway, proved quite satisfactory. As he himself records in 1840, "they all gave every one general satisfaction. We could now calculate with some certainty, not only upon the speed they could run, but also upon their not breaking down upon the journey"—a casualty which had previously been of not unfrequent occurrence. Sixty miles an hour, with good loads, was the speed to which they were equal.

In November of this year Sir Daniel took out a patent for steeling the surface of rails and tires. The invention was largely used. It was, he says, used exclusively on the Great Western engines and tenders, with great economy in the result. The use of any patented invention of his own by an official in the works of the Company to which he belongs

is sure to create jealousy and misrepresentation. Sir Daniel
seems to have suffered in this way. He found, he says, so
much trouble connected with his patent, "and the false
position I felt placed in with our own Company, that I
never took out another, nor do I ever approve of engineers
who advise large companies being themselves interested in
patents." Like Mr. Brunel and many other men of science,
he had formed and maintained to the last an unfavourable
opinion as to the general effect of the patent laws upon the
progress of invention, and the real interests of inventors.

With a view to the extension of the Great Western system
by the leases which had been taken of the Bristol and Exeter
and Swindon and Cheltenham Railways, the necessity had
become apparent in 1840 for the establishment of extensive
works for the manufacture and repair of their rolling stock. Mr.
Brunel approved of Sir Daniel's suggestion of Swindon as the
site, which, as situated at the junction with the Cheltenham
branch, would be most convenient as a centre from which
the engines could be worked. What were then green fields are
now covered with a flourishing town and works of enormous
magnitude, from which the engines, carriages, and waggons
required for working the two thousand five hundred miles of
the Great Western system are supplied.

The moving spirit in the organizing of this vast
establishment, as well as in developing the growth and
prosperity of the town of Swindon, was Sir Daniel Gooch. To
the end of his life his interest in the welfare of all connected
with the place never flagged. He took an active part in the
establishment of schools and libraries, and in providing those
reasonable amusements for vacant hours, the want of which
he had seen to be productive of so much injury in other
manufacturing centres. He was surrounded there by a highly
intelligent class of working-men, and he kept his hold upon

their respect and regard by his superior knowledge of the crafts in which they were engaged, and by his sympathy with every effort for their benefit, physical and mental. He had his reward in being selected to represent them in Parliament for over twenty years. Pronounced Conservative as he was, they felt how thoroughly he understood the interests of the working-classes, and how sincere was his wish to help them in every reasonable way. He was a man, as they well knew, who did not court popular applause, and was not given at any time to much speaking. Accordingly, they did not complain that he took no part in the debates. They respected him as a man of deeds, not of words, and were content to know that his services and his votes were always available in the public interest. In recording the close of his parliamentary career with the Dissolution in November 1885, he says, "I have taken no part in any of the debates. It would be a great advantage to business if there were a greater number of people who followed my example"—a view which must have been strongly confirmed by the incidents of the subsequent sessions.

Years of active association in the development of the Great Western system had deepened the mutual respect and regard which, from the first, had existed between Mr. Brunel and himself. No one could know that great engineer without admiration of his urbane and amiable character, no less than of his genius. Sir Daniel deeply appreciated both, and threw himself with hearty zeal into Mr. Brunel's plans for steamers of then unusual size for the improvement of the Atlantic service. The history of the *Great Western*, launched in 1837, the first steamship which made regular voyages across the Atlantic, is well known. The *Great Britain*, launched in 1843, the first large iron steamship, and the first large ship in which the screw-propeller was used, was at the time considered to be a monster ship, and thought by many to be doomed to certain failure. These predictions were disproved by several successful voyages to America, and by the manner in which she withstood the action of the sea during a whole winter after she had been run aground in Dundrum Bay. His experience of the perfect fitness of steamers of great size for ocean service emboldened Mr. Brunel to carry his experiments still further, and he projected the *Great Eastern* on a scale of magnitude, which no engineer of less daring than himself would then have dreamed to be practicable. So great was the confidence in the soundness of his views, that a company for building her was quickly formed. Mr. Brunel did not live to see the fulfilment of his plans. He died in September 1859, but it was the summer of the following year before the *Great Eastern* was ready for her first voyage across the Atlantic. The death of his dear friend seemed to have made Sir Daniel feel it to be a point of duty to watch over the fortunes of the vessel which that friend's genius had planned, and whose chequered fate in the difficulties which arose in getting her launched had no doubt helped in breaking down his health. Sir Daniel took an active interest in the completion of the vessel, and went out to New York with her on her first voyage in June 1860, when she made the run at the rate of 330 knots a day.

The vessel was a magnificent conception, but accident after accident interfered to mar her success as a commercial speculation. The vast sum sunk in her by the shareholders was lost, and the bondholders took possession of her in 1863. As a passenger-ship her career was ended. But she was destined before long to be the vehicle for laying the first successful Atlantic cable, a work of world-wide importance, which Sir Daniel records it as his conviction could not have been accomplished without her.

An unsuccessful attempt had already been made to lay a cable between England and America. The company by whom it had been undertaken could not find the money for a renewal of the attempt. In this state of affairs it was proposed, in 1864, to form a new company with sufficient capital to purchase the works of Messrs. Glass & Elliott, by which they would be able to make their own cable, and to undertake a contract for laying it. In this company Sir Daniel became a partner, taking £20,000 in shares. This the wealth which he had by this time acquired easily enabled him to do, the Directors of the Great Western Railway having many years before permitted him to engage in any other work which did not interfere with his duties to them. The attention of his partners and himself had naturally been turned to the *Great Eastern* as especially fitted for the operation of laying the cable. The company owning her had been wound up. To the bondholders, who had risked £100,000 upon her, she was a white elephant. Three of their number, who held the great proportion of her bonds, of whom Sir Daniel was one, resolved to purchase her, if they could, for £80,000. But, to their surprise, when she was put up for sale by auction in Liverpool, she was knocked down to them for only £25,000. A company to work the great ship was then formed, of which Sir Daniel was elected chairman, and a contract was made, chartering the vessel to lay the Atlantic cable, with the Telegraph Construction Company, of which, as already mentioned, he was also a director. Into this great enterprise he threw himself with all his wonted energy, devoting much time to looking after the construction of the cable, and also to the preparation of the *Great Eastern* for receiving it and paying it out.

In this way the best part of his leisure during the six months that he still remained in the service of the Great Western

Railway Company was spent. Having made a fortune amply sufficient for his desires, he had for some time meditated retiring in August 1862 from the position he had held there for twenty-five years. Attachment to those with whom he had worked so long induced him to protract his stay. Other men with other views of railway policy had now obtained influence in the Company. Mr. Charles Russell had been for some years dead. Mr. Ponsonby, now Lord Bessborough, and Mr. Walpole, his successors in the chair, had both resigned, and the retirement of its secretary, Mr. Charles Saunders, to whom Sir Daniel was warmly attached, as indeed were all who ever worked with him or under him, seems to have made Sir Daniel determine to send in his resignation. "We had worked together for nearly my whole life," he writes, "and never had a disagreement." The remark will be well understood by all who had the happiness of knowing Mr. Saunders either in his official capacity or as a friend. The public, too, owe that gentleman a debt of gratitude, for he impressed upon the whole staff connected with the railway that spirit of obliging courtesy of which travellers by it from the first felt the advantage, and of the traditions of which they continue still to reap the benefit.

Sir Daniel left the Great Western Railway in September 1864, to the general regret of all his colleagues and subordinates. He was presented, on the 3rd of June 1865, with an address from the officers and servants of the Company. In what he says of this incident the character of the man is well shown. "Man can receive no higher reward on earth than that of the goodwill and esteem of those with whom he has been associated through life, and my life had been passed in daily communication, both as master and brother officer, with those who gave expression to their feelings on this occasion. I count this 3rd of June as the brightest day in my life."

He had been invited to stand for Cricklade at the next election, which was then imminent, and would probably come off in his absence, as he had resolved to go out for the laying of the cable in the *Great Eastern*. The good will he had established at Swindon was speedily shown in the zeal with which a committee of the workmen there assisted his canvas. They did their work well in his absence. The nomination took place on the 12th of July, by which time he was on board the ship to whose destinies he was so devotedly attached, hoping for her, to use his own words, "a useful future, which should lift her out of the depression under which she had laboured from her birth, and satisfy him that he had done wisely in never losing confidence in her." How thoroughly that confidence was maintained will be seen from the vivid records in his diary of the countless difficulties and adventures which were encountered, and finally overcome, in laying the first working telegraphic cables in the depths of the great Atlantic sea.

Sir Daniel was returned for Cricklade on the 13th July 1865 by a considerable majority. The equanimity with which he competed for the honour shows itself very notably in his diary. On the 12th he writes, "I have often wondered whether my absence will have any effect upon the result." The great problem of which he was bent on seeing the solution interested him far more, for he adds, "Yet, if I knew it would have, I am certain I would have been here all the same. There is no comparison between the importance of the two works." Again, when informed of his success, "Has it in any way satisfied my ambition? I say no, for I do not feel I ever had any particular ambition for the honour. I value it chiefly for the warm-hearted feelings it has called forth in those who have been associated with me for a long, long time, and it is a sequel to the kind reception given to me a little while ago; but I look back upon that reception as more honourable than this. . . . What a change in one's life may be produced by a few hours! All the morning my mind has been very anxious. Now it is at rest, and I have only one anxiety left, viz., the success of the cable, the most important of all."

Much was to be undergone and a fresh voyage to be made before that success was ensured; but, by the 27th of July 1866, the cable was laid from the *Great Eastern*, and telegrams were flashed through it from shore to shore, the raising of the first cable, which had snapped at one of the deepest parts of the Atlantic, being postponed till this was done. By the end of the first week of September the end of the broken cable was recovered, united, and in working order. "What," the diary says, "will they now say in England, those who told me so often I was mad to hope to recover last year's cable from the deep Atlantic? . . . I know of nothing in the course of my life in which I have taken so deep an interest—an interest more intense than I will ever allow myself to take again in any enterprise." This feeling will come home to every one who follows the diarist through the day-by-day record of his exciting alternations of hope, anxiety, despondency, and triumph.

The progress of the enterprise had been watched by England with eager interest; for its importance in the interests of commerce and of international friendliness, as well as of science, was even then capable of being measured by every educated man. Sir Daniel had looked to success as his best reward, and was taken by surprise when, immediately upon his return to England, he was offered a Baronetcy—"a fate," he says, "which had certainly never entered my head . . . When all equally did their best, it seemed unfair that a few should be selected for any special reward."

Meanwhile an honour which probably came nearer to his heart had been conferred upon him. Since he left the Great Western Company in 1864, its affairs, which for some years before had been far from flourishing, had fallen into a very unsatisfactory state. Heavy liabilities had been undertaken, which the revenues of the Company were unable to meet. The value of its stock had sunk to a level calamitous to the shareholders, and it became clear that wise and energetic measures, in pursuance of a more enlightened and practical policy, could alone save the undertaking from disaster. For this task the tact, sagacity, and experience of a man conversant with the working of railways and with the conduct of great enterprises was necessary. Such a man seemed to present himself in the great mechanical engineer who had so long been connected with the undertaking, and by general consent he was invited to become Chairman of the Company. On the 2nd of March 1866 he presided, for the first time, over the general meeting of the shareholders, who gave him, as he records, "a kind and hearty reception." The reception grew warmer as he stated the principles on which he meant to act, viz., "to avoid all further obligations with new lines and extensions; to make, as far as possible, friendly relations with adjoining companies, and to cut down all capital expenditure to a minimum." In his capacity as Chairman of the Company, I had frequent opportunities professionally of observing with what calm and far-seeing sagacity these principles were carried out, and how admirably they were seconded by the able men who acted under his guidance. The effect soon became perceptible. Confidence, which had been shaken in the inherent value of the undertaking, began to be restored. Economy in working, at no sacrifice of efficiency, was established; attention was given to developing the traffic resources of the districts already occupied by the Company; unprofitable competition ceased, all unnecessary expenditure in extensions was avoided, and the numerous varieties of the Company's capital stock were consolidated. The benefit of these changes was felt in the gradual extinction of floating debt and the rise in the Company's dividends. Sir Daniel devoted himself to the onerous task he had undertaken with the same constancy and quiet perseverance for which he was distinguished through the earlier part of his career, only allowing himself the recreation, for such it was to him, of seeing another Atlantic cable laid from his beloved *Great Eastern* in 1869. In March of that year he had the satisfaction of announcing to the Great Western proprietary a dividend at the rate of 3¾ per cent., the highest that had been earned for eighteen years, which was followed in April 1872 by a dividend at the rate of 5⅜ per cent. The price of the shares, which had been £90 when he first took the chair, had now risen to £120, and the shareholders showed their appreciation of his services by voting him a honorarium of £5000. From this time onward the affairs of the Great Western Company continued to prosper under his guidance. The mixed gauge was laid throughout the greater part of the system. "Thus," he writes in October 1874, "is the poor broad gauge gradually dying out," and he calmly anticipates the time, not long distant, when it would be no more. Meanwhile the system continued to grow in magnitude, till it came to be composed, as it now is, of a greater number of miles than any other railway in the kingdom.

The great work of the tunnel, upwards of four miles long, under the River Severn, engaged much of Sir Daniel's attention, and from the serious difficulties which attended its construction, and the consequent cost, caused him no little anxiety during the latter years of his life. The increase of the actual cost over the original estimate, from £900,000 to more than £1,600,000, was calculated to daunt a man of less robust faith than his in the ultimate value to the Company of the enterprise when completed—a faith which, it may be said in passing, has been fully justified by the revenue it has already secured. In December 1886 he had the happiness to see the tunnel completed for passenger traffic, and to know that a boon of the greatest magnitude had thus been conferred upon the commercial and travelling public.

The shadows were now beginning to close round a long and crowded life. The friends who had "wrought and thought with him" were falling around him thick and fast, either into the grave or into the retirement which they had honourably earned. His diary teems with records of these losses, which weighed heavily on a man of his friendly and constant nature. Of these, perhaps the heaviest loss came suddenly upon him in the death, in September 1887, of his devoted friend and fellow-worker, Mr. James Grierson, who had since 1863 acted as the General Manager of the Great Western Company, and had won for himself a foremost place in the railway world, not more by his exceptional ability and energy than by the tact and fairness of the spirit which marked all his conduct. They thoroughly understood each other, and on Mr. Grierson he could rely with confidence, that the policy on which their minds were at one should be carried out with skill and decision. Sir Daniel's words in recording Mr. Grierson's death speak volumes as to what he felt: "His loss to me and to the railway interest cannot be replaced."

The labours of Sir Daniel's long and active life had now begun to tell upon him, but he remained at his post as Chairman of the Great Western. From that he could not be spared; but he felt himself much alone, with some of the men no longer beside him on whom he had come to lean in the management of this great undertaking. The energy of quiet enthusiasm which had carried him through his toilsome and honourable career began to flag, and health failed. In February 1889 he presided for the last time at the general meeting of the Great Western shareholders, when he had the satisfaction, of which he might well be proud, of announcing to them a dividend of no less than 7¼ per cent. The effort to fill the chair tried him, and from that time he had to give more thought than an actively minded man willingly gives to the care of his health. All that watchful affection could do to lighten the pains of weakness was done for him. He bore his illness, which brought him much suffering, with the patience of a man who throughout his life had recognised with gratitude the blessings which had crowned his efforts, and was content to lay down its burden whenever the call should come. It came on the 15th of October 1889, and he was buried in Clewer churchyard, near the pleasant home where his happiest hours had for many years been spent.

Of his professional abilities his works are the best memorial. He had that modest estimate of himself which is generally the concomitant of real power. Of speech he was chary, and his general demeanour was marked by that reserve of manner which is often mistaken for coldness. He was a man such as Wordsworth speaks of in the lines—

> You must love him ere to you
> He will seem worthy of your love.

But by those who knew him well, his kindness of heart, his sincerity in friendship, his high sense of duty, and the strong element of enthusiasm for what was beautiful or grand in nature, in art, or in character, he was loved, and his loss was recognised, as he himself would have wished it to be, by all whom he had himself loved or held in esteem.

T.M.

The following selection from Sir Daniel Gooch's Diaries has been made by his widow, with the assistance of personal friends who knew him well.

I

EARLY LIFE
1816–1837

LONDON, *December* 1867.
HER MAJESTY HAVING by Royal Letters Patent conferred upon me the rank and dignity of a Baronet, I feel it may not be uninteresting to those who succeed me in the Baronetcy, and to others, to know something of the life of him upon whom the title was first conferred.

Looking back, as I now do, for a period of thirty-five years, during which I have had to struggle with the world, I must first express my gratitude to God for the many and great blessings He has bestowed upon me. I feel and acknowledge that all is due to His goodness, and that many who have run the race of life with me, while falling greatly short in the result, have equally merited advancement.

The principle which has guided me through life has been a steady perseverance in the path of duty to my employers, not being disheartened by a first failure, but ever believing in the possibility of ultimate success, and a determination not to be led into changes by the inducement of immediate advancement. I feel proud of the thought that since I was a boy I have only been in one service, although I was on several occasions tempted by the offers of a higher salary to make a change. But some words my father once used to me have ever been present with me, "A rolling stone gathers no moss." The experience of my life has fully supported the truth of this saying, and I would earnestly urge it upon my children and young people to adopt it as their motto. Although I feel it is not possible for all men to succeed in life, yet I am sure few need fail to do well, if they win for themselves a character for strict honesty; and by this I do not merely mean that they will not steal, but that in their dealings with other men they will act with honour, not seeking to obtain an advantage by either suppressing or magnifying the truth, but conducting themselves in such a way that a feeling may be created in the minds of those with whom they are brought into contact, that what they say may be relied upon, and will honourably be fulfilled. This is the character which begets the confidence and esteem of the outer world. Make your immediate employers or associates feel that, having embarked with them in their enterprise, you can be relied upon steadily to persevere in the pursuit of their interest, and so identify yourself with them that they can rest assured you are not ever seeking for a change, because you thus might earn a few pounds a year extra. Be sure, as a general rule, your interests are in the end best promoted by such a course; it may be in some cases you will not be so rich, but you will be more esteemed.

It ought to be every man's greatest happiness and pride to say, "I have been associated with the same men through life." And to my mind, nothing speaks stronger against a man than for him, in describing his past life, to go through a long list of changes in his business associations, in the end trusted by none and esteemed by few. I earnestly pray that my children and their children may avoid this, and pursue that straight and certain path I have before described.

About the year 1827, my father, assisted by Mr. Hodgson, the historian of Northumberland, took great pains and expended much labour in tracing the pedigree of my family in the female line down to that period. I believe the cause of this was the restoration of the estates to some of the Border families that had been forfeited for rebellion and other political causes. I know that one case in which my father took much interest, and I believe spent some money, was that of an old man living in Bedlington as a labourer, who was thought to be the rightful owner of large estates of the Ford family. He, however, did not succeed; but the searching into pedigrees in this case induced my father to look into the matter for our own family, and he was greatly assisted by Mr. Hodgson. This pedigree, together with such records of the family as my father collected, are now entered in my large Family Bible. It shows that in the female line the family is of no mean descent, but may claim the blood of Alfred the Great. The portraits, as far back as Mr. Justice, are now in the family, the property of my eldest brother. The pedigree in the male line has not been investigated, but I hope, when I have a little leisure, to be able to do this. As far as it has gone, it is a Suffolk family. My father and mother were first cousins; in this way both had the blood of the female line.

I was born at Bedlington in Northumberland on the 24th day of August 1816. I have often heard my mother say my birth occurred about three o'clock in the morning, during an awful thunderstorm. My father had then lived in Bedlington about a year. He was engaged in the Bedlington Ironworks, at that time the property of my second cousins, the Langridges, and Mr. Sorden of Linden. The village of Bedlington was a tolerably clean and large country village, with half a dozen good houses in it.

We moved from this house to another near it when I was probably about three years old, as I can remember my trying to carry part of my cot over the street. I certainly was not more than three years old at the time, and I was only four years of age when I went to school. How well I remember the first day I was led there by the servant, and also the appearance of the two ladies who kept it. The ladies were a Miss Robson and her sister, Miss Betsey. They must have been kind to me, as I was very fond of them, and long after looked back upon them as old friends. My mother has often told me I was sent so early to school, as I was rather inclined to keep the house in hot water by my mischievous pranks. I do not know exactly how long I was at that school, but probably a few years, as the next I went to was at Mr. Thompson's, the clergyman of Horton parish, who lived at a place called Condhall, nor far from Cramlington, and about four miles from Bedlington. It was a large school. The boys were chiefly the sons of farmers living round about; and, as most of us rode there on donkeys or ponies, probably some thirty of those animals were congregated in the old buildings used as stables at the school. We all had a great regard for Mr. Thompson, and also for Mrs. Thompson. Both were very kind to us. We dined in the schoolroom, where Mrs. Thompson looked after us, and did all she could for our comfort. We used to have each a large basin of milk, and I well remember the thick coating of cream upon it, into which we used to dip our bread. I even now look back upon the time I was at that school as a very happy period in my life.

Mr. Thompson was very indulgent, and often when the Northumberland pack of foxhounds, then belonging to Sir Matthew White Ridley, came past the place, he did not punish us if we mounted our steeds and went after them.

It was a great amusement for the gentlemen hunting to see some eighty donkeys and ponies and us boys. There were also times when Mr. Thompson had either a wedding or a funeral to attend to at his church, which was a couple of miles from the school; and in his absence his eldest son used to take charge of the school, but, not being much older than the eldest of the boys, he had not very much command of us, and we used to have all kinds of fun in the school, shutting the shutters to prevent people outside seeing what we were about. We thought little and cared little about the loss of time in our studies. My chief playmate was George Marshall, who lived at Bedlington. He was the son of a widow, farming their own farm, and he had a sweet girl as his sister, who died, as I well remember, further on. He and I were inseparable companions; our evenings and our Saturdays (on which day there was no school) were always spent together, although I do not think there was a great similarity in our dispositions. He was quieter, had less mischief in him, and I believe most of the scrapes he got into were through my leading. His mother was very kind to me, and treated me as she did her own son. For some time we used to ride together on the same pony to school. My Saturdays were always spent either on the farm, or at the collieries or iron-works. I used to go often to a pit called the Glebe, and nothing pleased me so much as going underground and driving the trams. In looking back at all the risks I ran at this pit, it is a wonder to me I never met with an accident; but it was not in my nature at that time to have any fear, and I could never rest an hour at home. My father was rather strict with us on Sunday. We went to church morning and afternoon, and at the afternoon service I, with the rest of the young people, had to say the Catechism before the congregation. We all stood in a circle round the reading-desk; for this a large open space in the church was well fitted, and the questions were put by Mr. Coates, the minister, a true pattern of a clergyman, a gentleman in every sense of the word, beloved by all. The church and churchyard at that time (it has since been much altered, I think, for the worse) were kept in the most beautiful order. It was the great pride of Mr. Coates to see the churchyard kept neat, and filled with flowers and pretty shrubs; and so much was he liked, that even we mischievous boys respected them for his sake, and never did them any harm, although we used often to play there, as it was always open. A grandson of Mr. Coates was also a playfellow of mine, and I used often to be at the Parsonage.

The old women of the village had a considerable dread of me, yet I believe they liked me all the better for the pranks I used to play upon them. One great amusement was to fill a cow's horn with old tar-rope, and then to put a hot cinder in it, and insert the small end of the horn into the keyhole, or any other opening we could get through the cottage door, and by blowing at the large end, driving the smoke into the cottage. This we called *funking* the old women, and it was generally a winter evening's amusement. There were no policemen in those days to protect the victims of the iniquity. There were, however, two very serious scrapes we got into, and for which we were threatened with the magistrate. George Marshall, Harry Coates, and myself found some young girls in one of Marshall's fields. We told them to go out, instead of doing which they laughed at us. I had at the time a small frog in my hand, and as one of them opened her mouth in laughing rather wide, I slipped the frog into it. She said it went down her throat, and they all went off screaming to the village. There was soon a hue and cry after us, and we had to keep out of the way until night. There was a general inquiry next day, and we were threatened with a visit to Morpeth jail, but somehow we got out of the scrape. I am not sure to this day whether she did or did not actually swallow the frog. Another serious scrape was our nearly hanging a boy. Four of us were playing in the rickyard at the back of Marshall's house. As the hayricks had just been put up, a ladder was standing up against one of them, and we proposed a game at hanging. I remember I was to be hanged *last*. Of course one boy had to be the first, so we got a small rope and fastened it round his neck, getting the other end over one of the rounds of the ladder, and so pulled him up off the ground. This end we made fast, and thought it good fun to see him kick his legs about. Fortunately we heard the bailiff coming, and all ran away. Still more fortunately he happened to go round and saw the boy hanging, and was just in time to get him down and save his life. He was black in the face and insensible. I have often thought since what a painful thing for us through life it would have been had we killed him. The poor boy carried the mark of the rope round his neck for some time afterwards, but in a few days we were playing together again, little feeling the escape we had all had. We got into considerable hot water about this.

Another amusement we used to have was for our school to challenge some other one to fight, for which we used to prepare ourselves with swords made of wood, and in these fights we got many very hard knocks. The last one I was at I was the captain, and the ground selected was a road leading from the bottom of the village to the ironworks, a high hedge on one side and a steep bank down to the river on the other side. The plan of battle was to force each other's ranks. Drawn up as we were across the road facing each other, this was a very hard battle and a drawn one. I am not sure we did not get the worst of it. It was to be renewed at another time, but this was prevented by the schoolmaster. Many swords were broken, and sundry combatants sent down the bank into the bushes. These amusements, if rough, I think did us no harm; they taught us a certain amount of self-reliance, and we never suffered any serious personal injury. Bedlington, at the time I was there, was often the scene of sharp fights between the excisemen and the smugglers, who used to carry whisky across the Scotch borders. These men used to ride generally a very good horse with kegs of whisky hung like saddle-bags on the saddle; and as the population of the village in all cases took the part of the smuggler, the excisemen often got the worst of it. I remember one night a very hard fight with two smugglers. The excisemen had got them off the horses, and secured the kegs of whisky, which they placed against the side of a house while they were securing the men, and we, finding the kegs, stove the ends in and let the whisky run to waste, much to the disgust of the excisemen when they came to take them away. I used to enjoy these rows. There was also great excitement in the village at the time of the Burke and Hare murders in Edinburgh. What were called resurrection-men used to rob the graves of the bodies for the doctors, and all that winter the churchyard was watched for some time after any one had been buried. Hare, who turned king's evidence, and was let off, was supposed to be at Bedlington one night; at any rate, a man believed to be he was there, and the whole place turned out to lynch him. It was a wonder he was not killed. Had he not possessed good legs he certainly would have been, but his fleetness enabled him to keep ahead of his pursuers, and they did not get hold of him, but pelted him with stones until he got away in the dark. He certainly was a bad-looking fellow. I had seen him in the afternoon begging. My father, as church-warden, and a constable used to go round to all the lodging-houses for tramps, to see who was in them at night, and I used often to accompany them.

It was a winter of great dread, which was made worse by many practical jokes,—by a piece of sticking plaster being put over people's mouths in the dark,—the belief being that a number of people were killed by the resurrection-men in that way, they having a plaster which the person operated on could not get off. I had a dagger made out of an old bayonet that I used to carry about with me when out after dark, although I daresay I should have used my legs freely had I fancied there was any real danger.

When ten or twelve years old, my father indulged my taste for mechanics by buying me a lathe and box of tools. The former I still have, or rather what is left of it, and I took lessons in turning. This was a source of great amusement and usefulness to me, as it caused me to think, and also to read useful books on mechanics. I acquired a considerable amount of skill in fancy turning, and got a great deal of employment from the ladies for screen handles, chessmen, &c. I collected all the large bones I could get to make things in bone. My father took a great deal of interest in what I did. He was very fond of a little carpentering himself, and had a good idea of mechanics, although he had received no mechanical training. I quite understood the details of the steam-engine; and, for a boy who had to depend upon himself, got from books and such experiments as I could make a fair knowledge of natural philosophy. Arnold was a very favourite book of mine. A plan I found very useful was to write down from memory what I had been reading. In science, to enable you to do this requires that you should understand fully what you have read, as you have to put it into your own language. I have ever looked back upon my years I spent at Bedlington as very happy ones. I know they have been very useful to me in after life, giving me a feeling of self-reliance which I have needed, having my way to fight in the world. My dear parents gave me all the education they could, and such as was to be obtained in private schools, and while leaving me much liberty, they set me a high example. I may say Sunday was the only day when my time was not at my own disposal out of school-time, and I often used to be out of the house on a Saturday morning before any one was up. I remember eating my breakfast before going to bed to save time next morning. Before I left Bedlington—I do not know in what year it was—I went to Morpeth to see a steam-engine working in the common road. It was built by Messrs. Hawthorne of Newcastle, and drew a threshing-machine after it; I believe it was for the Duke of Northumberland. It was on its way from Newcastle to Alnwick. I found it at a stand, owing to some defect, on a hill a little before reaching Morpeth, but I waited to see it repaired, and went on with the driver, making the turnings of the streets capitally. It made a strong impression on me. I knew all about the iron horses, as they were then called, on the waggon-way. George Stephenson was frequently at my father's house, and used to take a great deal of notice of me by taking me on his knee and talking to me about pits, &c. At that time he was much engaged in advising on colliery matters, and had just commenced his glorious career. My eldest brother Tom went to his works at Newcastle as a pupil. Mr. Locke (afterwards celebrated as a railway engineer) was also there, and used frequently to come to Bedlington to spend his Sunday with my brother. I well remember the discussions about railways, then called waggon-ways, and the first introduction of the long straight iron rail. Mr. Birkenshaw, the manager of the Bedlington Rails Works, took out a patent for making these rails— fish-bellied, as they were called, the chairs or supports being placed at the weak part of the rail and the bellied part giving strength between. It was at that time a great advance in the art of rolling to give this varying depth of bar. Amongst my father's papers I found the annexed slip, showing that he foresaw the great future in railways from the introduction of these straight iron rails. He lived to see some considerable progress made:—

"The only manufactory in this parish is that carried on under the firm of —— & Co., the leading feature in which is the manufactory of railway bars invented by Mr. Baker, for which he obtained a patent, an improvement as connected with the present prospects of railways becoming of general use, from which the most beneficial results may be expected, both from their superior durability of metal as well as from the facility given to locomotion from the lengths (from 15 to 18 feet) in which they can be laid down without a joint."

Since writing the above I found, on making an inspection of the lines of the Great Western Railway at Stratford-upon-Avon, these rails laid on an old line purchased by the Great Western Company between Stratford-on-Avon and Morton, and learned from Mr. S——, whose father was instrumental in laying the road, that the present rails were originally obtained from Bedlington in the year 1830. The line is worked by trains, and the rails are still in good order (1867). I have had a sample sent to me to keep as a relic of the early history of railways. This is now at Clewer, and it ought to be preserved.

In February 1831 my father left Bedlington to go to Tredegar Ironworks in Monmouthshire, and took his family with him. I remember well what a pleasant journey it was. He had a kind of omnibus built with curtains round it, in which we all travelled, posting. I do not know how many days it took us to make the journey, but I well remember it, and the beautiful view as we crossed the Malvern Hills. It was a bright moonlight evening. When we were settled at Tredegar,

I began my professional career by working in the works. Mr. Samuel Humfray was the managing partner. I went first into the moulding department, commencing work at six o'clock in the morning. The first few months I was chiefly employed in making cores, but after that was intrusted to mould tram-wheels. This was a very heavy job for me. The wheel pattern weighed 50 or 60 lbs., and I had nine boxes to mould twice a day, the first lot before nine o'clock in the morning, when the furnace was run off and they were cast. During this time I went to my breakfast for a couple of hours, when I returned and opened the boxes, tempered my sand, and moulded the second set; this was generally finished between four and five o'clock. I had an hour for dinner. As this work was done in the atmosphere of the furnace-house, and the work was very hard, I began to feel the effects of it in my health, and was sent a voyage to sea for a few months. I went to Bristol and got a passage in a ship going to Liverpool and back. This was the first time I was in Liverpool. My brother John was at this time in Warrington, and I went to him to spend the few days the ship was unloading, and loading to return. On my return to Tredegar, I went into the pattern shop, and did not do any more moulding. The foreman of the moulders, Ben Williams, was very kind to me, and gave me all the information he could. I also obtained from those working the furnaces a good deal of information as to the mode of working them, and learned to know from the cinder and other indications the quality of the iron produced. Here also my system of writing down any facts I collected was of great use, as it not only stimulated me to collect such facts, but impressed them more strongly on my mind. Several of my books of notes are still in my possession. The foreman in the pattern-shop was a Mr. Ellis; his son was the engineer of the works—that is, had charge of all the mechanical department. Old Ellis, as we used to call him, was somewhat of a character; but he was always a kind friend to me, and gave me any information he could. He had a book with a store of facts valuable at the time as the result of a life's experience, and this was always at my service. He gave me a pearl-handle knife, which I still have. One of the men in the shop was also most kind to me—his name was Jonathan Miles—taking great pains to instruct me in the proper use of my tools and assisting me in every way he could. I am glad to feel that I have since that time had it in my power to return some of his kindness by giving him employment at Swindon, where he has been for a great many years, respected by all his fellow-work men. He is now, in 1867, a very old man, and not able to do much; but he still is at the bench, and is very sensitive about his ability to do as much as ever he used to do. Poor old Jonathan! I shall feel as though I had lost a friend when it pleases God to take you. We worked very much together at Tredegar.

One of the duties of our shop was to repair the valves of the blowing-engine. They were made of wood faced with leather, and one or other of the engines had to be done every Saturday morning. I always went to this work, as it took me amongst the engines, and we often had some excitement in performing the duty. This on two occasions was made rather too strong. There were three large blowing-engines at Tredegar at that time, and they were all connected by the blowing-pipes, so that in case of accident to one engine the others could blow the furnaces. Each engine had a large regulator, or sort of iron balloon, to equalise the blast from the varying strength of the cylinders. To make their regulators tight, it was the practice to put powdered lime into them. A young fellow, a little older than myself, of the name of Jenkins, and I were inside the blowing-cylinders, putting on a new valve, when one of the firemen near lifted

the valve between our engine and the next one, when the
blast came through the regulator upon us, bringing with it
the lime-powder, and we could not get out, for the pressure
shut the valves where we were; but as one was off in another
place, the engine-house was also soon filled with lime, and
the engineer, knowing where we were, and what had been
done, ran as hard as he could to shut off the valve again,
and returned to find us nearly dead from suffocation. A
very little more, and it would have been all over with us. We
thought at the time the furnaceman did it on purpose, as
he knew we were there, and he had no business in any case
to lift the valve. The old scamp! we played him some tricks
for it afterwards, gave a dog his dinner, watered his beer,
and all the other men about the furnace condemned him,
and gave us every opportunity of clearing off scores with
him. Another occasion was, I believe, quite accidental, but
the result of carelessness, although the engineer was a great
friend of mine and a good fellow. We were in the bottom
of the cylinder, and had just finished the work; one of the
men had gone out, and we were just about to follow, when
we were much astonished to see the engine start. The piston
at the time was about half stroke, so that we could stand
nearly upright; fortunately it made its first start upwards,
or we would have been flattened like a cake between it and
the bottom of the cylinder. Before it had time to make the
up-stroke and return, we were able to crouch down into the
square valve box at the bottom (these tubes being about two
feet square and the same depth, just enough to crouch into),
when down came the piston again within an inch or so of
our heads. Fortunately the man who had left us was in the
engine-house, and shouted to the engineer, who stopped the
engine at once, before she could make another upstroke, or I
fear the valves would have given us a hard squeeze. It was not

at all uncommon for us to sit in these valve-boxes when the engine was moved a little, but then we either had the valve off or made fast. I must say, it was a curious sensation to be there, and hear the roar of the air rushing in, as the piston moved, or on the piston coming down upon us, shutting us up in this little tube until it moved up again. With all this, I used to like those Saturday mornings in the blowing-engines; and, as that liking was not general in the shop, it was readily accorded to me. A boy was also a better size for the confined space than a man, if they could depend upon him to do the work properly. I therefore took it as a compliment to me that I was so much trusted. I also had a very narrow escape when erecting a roof over the rolling-mill. We were putting up a new one just over the large fly-wheel—a very improper thing to be allowed to do when the mill was at work, as, if we happened to fall, nothing could save us amongst those great wheels. One morning while we were at breakfast, the fly-wheel broke and flew through the roof we were at work upon, carrying everything away before it. Half an hour later, and we would have gone with it. I worked upon the iron roof of the market-house, and, as it was put up during the winter, it was a dreadfully cold job. I have looked on it on the occasions I have been at Tredegar since, and recalled my feelings in those cold days. I think on one occasion I saved the life of my brother William. He was a little fellow, and had gone with me to the works. I missed him from the shop, and went out to look for him, when I saw him standing between the rails of a road that passed the end of the shop. On going towards him, I saw a locomotive coming within a very few yards, of which he was taking no notice, and had just time to run and pull him out of the way. It made my heart jump, and was a very narrow escape for him. Fortunately, the engines on these roads did not travel very fast.

Mr. Bevan and Mr. Jones, the mineral agents, were also very kind to me. Although only a boy, they always gladly told me anything I wished to know about the mines, and allowed me to go with them sometimes. Large works of this kind are by far the best school for a young engineer to get a general knowledge of what he needs in after life. It is, in fact, the foundation for all else. Every Englishman ought to know and understand the manufacture of iron and working of mines. It is a kind of knowledge that is constantly coming in useful as he gets older, and I look back upon the time spent at Tredegar as by far the most important years of my life, and will ever feel grateful to those, many in number, who were so kind to me in enabling me to obtain and in giving me information. It was also at Tredegar where the delight of having earned money for myself was first felt by me, a feeling that cannot come twice in a man's life. Those first few sovereigns gave me more pleasure than millions could do now. When I first went to work, the important question of my wages took some time to settle, and it was nearly four months before finally an arrangement was made. I had sixteen weeks pay due to me, and the amount per week being 9s., I was indeed a proud boy as I walked away from the pay-table with upwards of £6 in my hand. I did not think there was so rich a person in the world. Oh, those first feelings of life, once passed never to return with equal force or earnestness!

About early in 1833 my father's health began to fail him. Although we had no idea of any danger, he went to London for advice, and stopped at my Uncle Robinson's at Worcester on his return, where my mother went to meet him. He was very weak, but quite cheerful. The evening before he died he sat up to the usual hour, then went to bed and fell asleep. A few hours afterwards my mother woke and found him dead

(August 28, 1833). It was a great and unexpected blow to us all. I went to Worcester, hoping to be in time to attend his funeral, but was too late, the funeral having taken place the day I reached there. My father was buried at a pretty country churchyard a little distance from Worcester called Claines, where his sons put up a monument to his memory a little later. I thus at a very early age lost a good father, and my poor mother was left to care for four others younger than myself, and nobly she performed her task. I had few companions at Tredegar. Two young surgeons, pupils of Mr. Jackson, who was the surgeon to the works, were the only young men I associated with. I spent a great deal of time with them at the surgery, and learned the arts of drawing teeth and making plaisters. I used sometimes to accompany them in their visits to the sick, and we often had some shooting together on the mountain. One was a nephew of Mr. Humfray, named Alfred Humfray, and the other a Mr. Fenton; both are since dead.

My mother remained in the town of Tredegar after the death of my father, and I continued at the works. During the time I was there the Merthyr riots took place; I forget the year. The Tredegar men did not join the rioters. On the Friday a large body of them, collected from Nantyglo and Ebbw Vale, passed through Tredegar on their way to join the Dowlais and Merthyr men, where they attacked the Castle Inn, in which a number of one of the Highland regiments and the magistrates were. The soldiers were obliged to fire from the windows upon the mob, and I think twenty-one men were killed. They were beaten off for the time, but determined to collect additional strength by the Monday. Early on the Monday morning a much larger number passed through Tredegar, and got hold of all the men they could to force them to go with them. I was amongst the unwilling ones, and

with the others was placed in front, the men behind having
sticks with spikes in the end to push us on. There were eight
or ten thousand altogether. When we got to Rhymney, we
saw a lot of soldiers drawn up along the ridge of Dowlais
Hill, instead of our meeting the Merthyr men there, as had
been arranged. A considerable amount of bluster took place
as they ascended the hill, we in the front not liking the look
of things at all. When we reached the soldiers, some of the
magistrates came forward to advise the men to disperse and
return home. This could not be listened to, and they would
march on to Merthyr in spite of the soldiers. The magistrates
then retired, and the soldiers were ordered to "present"—
unpleasant sound to us in front, as one word of command
received, and who could say how many of us would roll in
the dust. A panic certainly took possession of us in the front,
and was as quickly communicated to those behind, and a
general scramble down the hill took place, so that in a very
few minutes the word "Fire" would have done us no harm.
The Tredegar people were right glad to get back, and we had
some revenge on our oppressors; as they in parties of two
and three passed back through Tredegar on their way home,
we gave them a fair amount of chaff. The soldiers managed
this matter very well, as they took possession of the hill first,
and so prevented the two bodies of men meeting. This put
an end to the riots. On the Friday the men disarmed a troop
of yeomanry coming up from Cardiff, I think, and got one
of the bayonets off the musket of one of the Highlanders
when they made a rush upon them at the Castle Inn. This
bayonet, with a small flag tied to it, was carried on a pike by
the party with whom I had the honour of marching. I have
often asked myself since whether I was really frightened at
the position I was in, but I think not. It is true the number
of lives lost on the Friday made me feel the soldiers would

fire if necessary, but I seemed to enter into the spirit of the march and the excitement of the shouting and noise, and I had no real occasion to get into the mess. Had I stayed at home I would not have done so, as they only went into the workmen's houses.[1]

Just before leaving Tredegar I did a very foolish thing. I was dared to go down a pit about thirty yards deep by the chain and come up in the same way. This I did. It was a balance pit with a large round link chain; I thought by taking a piece of iron to put through the links to rest on I could manage it easily: I went down easily enough, and had no difficulty for more than half the distance in coming up; but as I got near the top I felt my muscular power failing me, and nothing but a struggle between life and death enabled me to hold on. My arms and legs began to tremble so, I could hardly hold to the chain, and I am sure if I had had a couple more yards to do before I reached the top, I must have given up and gone crash to the bottom. It was a lesson I never forgot, and therefore it had its use. I saw a man a year ago on board the *Great Eastern* in a similar predicament. He was sent up a rope to free a line, and before he could get back his muscles gave out, and but for Halpin going up after him and supporting him on his shoulders down again, the man must have fallen down into the paddle engine-room. But he shouted at the top of his voice; I made no noise, but felt death almost certain.

The time for leaving Tredegar now arrived, and I left it with a heavy heart. I had been very happy there, and liked not to part with old friends. One of my best and dearest friends gave me, the night before I left, a small Bible and Prayer-book, which I have deeply valued, and ever will value so long as life lasts, telling me ever to seek in it comfort and support in all my trials through life. I have never forgotten those kind words, and I pray God they may not have been used in vain. We travelled from Tredegar in the carriage which was used to take us there from Bedlington. My mother went to live at Coventry, in a house about a mile out of the town. I stayed there until I left for the Vulcan Foundry.

On 28th January 1834 I left home to go and work at the Vulcan Foundry, near Warrington, in Lancashire, under Mr. Robert Stephenson. He and Mr. Tayleur of Liverpool had just built their works—indeed they were not quite finished—when I went there. They were intended chiefly for building locomotives. This was the first time I had left my home, and my dear mother gave me much good advice, which has been of use to me through life. I remember well her telling me always to keep my thoughts fixed on obtaining for myself a good position in life, never to be satisfied to stand still; and although I was going to the Vulcan as a boy and a pupil, to strive to one day become the manager. I have often in after life thought over my mother's words, and seen the wisdom of them. The road to success in life is open to all who will with determination and honour follow it, never looking back, but keeping the eyes and soul ever fixed forward. Men are more indebted to their mothers, I think, for the feelings and impressions that guide them through life than they are to their fathers. There is more of sympathy between the boy and his mother than with the father; the advice is probably given more in love and less as a duty from her, and comes nearer home to the heart of the boy, while from the father it appeals more to the reason; and all who have lived fifty years, feel and know how much greater and purer the heart is with us than the reason. I left my mother's roof with great regret. I was going out alone into an unknown world, amongst strangers, and I quite well remember I did not feel very happy. I arrived at the Newton Junction late in the evening, and found Mr. Charles Tayleur, the manager of the Vulcan Works, in the waiting-room. I had a letter from Mr. Stephenson for him, and presented it with great awe to him, as the arbitrator of my future. He, however, spoke in a kind, friendly way to me, and this did much to reassure me. Lodgings had been taken for me at a farmhouse close to Newton Junction, called the Moss.

The works were situated about a mile from the Moss, down a wretched dirty lane with ruts a foot deep. I had to be in the works not later than ten minutes past six in the morning, and a dreadful walk it was in the dark when I first went there. As we were only allowed half an hour for breakfast, I was obliged to take my breakfast with me, consisting of a can of new milk and bread and butter. This I used to eat in the stationary engine-room. Being allowed an hour for dinner, I was able to walk up to the Moss, and get that meal very comfortably, but it did not give me a very long time. I worked very hard at these works. A man of the name of Ireland (who is now old, but is still at the Vulcan) and I used to take jobs on piece-work together, and both worked hard. I was much indebted to Ireland. He was a well-informed and respectable man, and gladly gave me all the instruction and assistance he could. I was always glad to go out with the new engines, and in this way was a good deal on the Liverpool and Manchester Railway, and became acquainted with Mr. Milling at the Liverpool end, and Mr. Fife at the Manchester end. They were the locomotive superintendents, and gave me facilities to ride about on the engines. I thus got a good deal of useful experience in the working of a railway, which I could not have got in the workshops alone. Mr. Tayleur was kind to me in this respect, as it was only by his permission I could get out of the factory. I knew some very nice families in Warrington, where I went occasionally to spend the

Saturday afternoon. Toward the middle of the summer my
health began to give way, and, after the doctor at Warrington
had doctored me for some time, I was obliged to give up
work and go home to Coventry early in September 1834. I
remained there until the end of the year. My brother Tom was
the engineer on that part of the London and Birmingham
Railway, and had his principal offices in Coventry. I used to
go there and draw most days, or went out on the trucks with
his assistants. This rest and my mother's care restored me to
health, and, instead of returning to Newton, I arranged to go
to the Dundee foundry at Dundee as a draftsman, the hard
work in the shops being considered more than my strength
could bear. I left home early in January 1835, and, on my way
to Dundee, paid a visit to G. Marshall at Bedlington, and
spent a few days in Edinburgh, arriving at Dundee on the
17th February.

The Dundee foundry did a class of work I had not before
had an opportunity of seeing, such as marine engines, flax
and other general machinery. Mr. James Stirling, now of
Edinburgh, was the chief manager, and I always found Mr.
Stirling very kind. I had the large salary of one pound per
week, and am glad to say I made this keep me, and thus
ceased to be any burden upon my mother, a matter that gave
me very great pleasure, as she could ill afford to help me.
Living at Dundee was very cheap. I was fortunate in having
in Dundee an old friend from Bedlington, a Mr. Nicholson,
who had been brought up at the Bedlington Ironworks, and
was then manager of the Dundee and Newtyle Railway.
He had married there. Mrs. Nicholson was a kind, good
woman, and I received both from Mr. and Mrs. Nicholson
the greatest kindness. I dined with them most Sundays, and
often spent the evenings with them; their house was almost
a home to me. The Sturrocks also lived here; Archie, who

afterwards served under me in the Great Western, and who was many years locomotive superintendent of the Great Western Railway, was serving his time at the foundry, so that I had plenty of pleasant society. There was a very good Mechanics' Institution here, of which I was a member, and attended the lectures regularly. The library was also a good one for such purposes.

For three or four years I had been a great believer in making use of the galvanic battery as a power instead of steam. When at Tredegar I tried a great many experiments, and there constructed a small engine to be worked by this power. It had a very short glass cylinder with straight iron ends, and I got my power by magnetising these cylinder curves alternately, and with a good heavy fly-wheel got a rotating motion.

As it was not my intention when I went to Dundee to stay there more than the year, I finished with the Foundry Company on the 31st December, and on the 6th January 1836 left all my kind friends in Dundee with very great regret. I had arranged with Mr. R. Stephenson to go to his works at Newcastle, and, after spending a little time at Edinburgh and Bedlington, reached Newcastle on the 26th January (1836), beginning my work at the works the following day. I got lodgings in Blackett Street. I did not stay in these lodgings, but joined Harry Birkinshaw (a son of the Mr. Birkinshaw of the Bedlington Ironworks) in some lodgings in Carliol Street, where I went on the 16th February. I had plenty of friends in Newcastle, and scarcely ever spent an evening at home, and generally went to the theatre one evening a week. My cousin, Mr. George Hawkes, was very kind to me, and my Sundays were often spent with them. My wages at the works were not large. To begin with, I had a pound a week when I was in the drawing-office; this, after a couple of months, was increased to thirty shillings, when I certainly felt myself very rich, and took an extra night at the theatre. I made some drawings for locomotive engines for Russia, which were oddly enough afterwards two engines on the Great Western Railway. The Russian railway was a six-feet gauge, and I was much delighted in having so much room to arrange the engine. For some financial reasons, all the engines we made were not sent out, and two of them were made with seven-feet gauge for the Great Western Railway, the "North Star," and the "Morning Star." I was very much impressed in making these drawings with the importance of a wider gauge, and no doubt thus early became an advocate for the broad gauge system, although at the time Mr. Brunel had not propounded his views on the subject,[2] and I did not foresee how important a matter it was to be in my future life. I occasionally at this time used to go over to Sunderland to spend the Sunday at John Wilkinson's, and I there met my wife for the first time at a party on the 25th of July 1836.

In September Mr. Robert Hawkes, who had taken great notice of me both while in Newcastle and when I lived at Bedlington—he used to be pleased with my skill in turning—asked me to go to their works at Gateshead. He proposed they should build a locomotive engine-works, and take me in as a partner in this department. This matter was so arranged, and I left Mr. Stephenson on the 8th of October, and went to the Gateshead works. They were then building a couple of locomotives for the Newcastle and Carlisle Railway. I was engaged in getting out plans for the new works, and looking after the engines then in hand. A Mr. Thompson was to join this new concern towards the end of the month. Thompson and I went south to buy machinery, and visited Leeds and Manchester. At this latter place I first became acquainted with

Mr. Whitworth. We ordered some tools from him. We spent a few weeks in visiting the various shops, and seeing my old friends in this part of Lancashire. When Thompson returned, Whitworth and I went to pay a visit at Tredegar, where I arrived on the 17th November, from whence I went on to Bristol to see Mr. Brunel, to try and get an order for some of the Great Western broad-gauge engines, which they had then determined upon building. I went to the Great Western Office, and saw the directors, as it happened to be a Board day, but found that Mr. Brunel was not in Bristol. I then went to Warwick to see my mother, she having removed from Coventry there. Here I was taken very unwell, and was detained until the second week in January 1837, when I returned to Newcastle. There is a great contrast in the travelling between that time and this. I left Coventry for Manchester at 8.30 at night, and ought to have arrived there between seven and eight next morning; but owing to the bad state of the road, did not reach it until three in the afternoon, or in nearly nineteen hours. It now takes a little over 2 hours to perform the same journey. On my arrival at Newcastle, I went to Bedlington. My brother Tom was then the engineer of the Manchester and Leeds Railway, and I at once went to ask him to give me something to do, and this he kindly did. I therefore left Newcastle and went to him at Rochdale on the 25th May, and began my work on that part of the railway. I went to the opening of the Grand Junction Railway on the 4th of June.

1. The account of this incident given in the "Annual Register" for June 1831 thus concludes:—"The Riot Act was read by a magistrate who accompanied the soldiers, and they were ordered to present their pieces, at the sight of which every man took to his heels and returned home."

2. They had, however, been communicated to the Directors of
    the Great Western Railway in October 1835.

II

THE GREAT WESTERN RAILWAY ENGINES AND THE BROAD GAUGE
1837–1859

Towards the end of July 1837 I heard that Mr. Brunel wanted some one to take the post of locomotive engineer on the Great Western Railway, and I at once went to him, on July 20th, preferring that department to railway making. The offices of the Grand Junction Railway were removed from Rochdale to Manchester at the end of the month, and I went to live there. I heard from Mr. Brunel on the 2nd of August, saying he was coming into the North, and that he would call and see me. This gave me some brighter hopes, and he called at the office on the 9th August, and arranged I should go to him at once. I was very glad of this appointment, as I felt it was a permanent thing, in which by attention and perseverance I might hope to get on. I was also very glad to have to manage the broad gauge, which filled my mind as the great advance of the age, and in the soundness of which I was a firm believer. I left Manchester and went to

Daniel Gooch in 1845

London, beginning my duties with the Great Western on the 18th August 1837. None of the engines had then been delivered, although several were ordered, six from the Vulcan Foundry, my old shop, four from Mather Dixon & Co. of Liverpool, and two from Sharp, Roberts, & Co., Manchester, two from Hawthorne & Co., Newcastle, and two from the Haigh Foundry Company, also the two altered Russian engines, before mentioned, from Robert Stephenson & Co., Newcastle. My first work was to prepare plans for the engine-houses at Paddington and Maidenhead, and I then went to inspect the engines then building. I was not much pleased with the design of the engines ordered. They had very small boilers and cylinders, and very large wheels. Those made by the Vulcan Company had wheels 8 feet in diameter, and three of them only 12-inch cylinders with 18-inches stroke; two of Mather Dixon's had 10-feet wheels and 14-inch cylinders, with very small boilers. Those made by Hawthorne were on a patent plan of Tom Harrison's, having the engine and boiler on separate carriages, and coupled with ball-and-socket steam-pipes. These were immense affairs; the boilers were large, and the cylinders were, I think, 16-inches diameter, and about 2-feet stroke. In one, the cylinders were coupled direct to the driving wheels, which were 10 feet diameter, and the other had a spur and pinion 3 to 1, with 6-feet wheel, making the wheel equal to 18 feet diameter. The same plan of gearing was used in the two engines built by the Haigh Foundry; their wheels were 6 feet diameter and the gearing 2 to 1, but the cylinders were small. I felt very uneasy about the working of these machines, feeling sure they would have enough to do to drive themselves along the road. The Great Western line had been laid out with very flat gradients, generally 4 feet per mile, and a maximum of 8 feet, with the exception of the inclines at Box and Wootton Bassett, which were 1 in 100. The idea was to concentrate the gradients on these inclines, and work them with stationary power. In the directors' report to the shareholders of the 25th August 1836 these matters are referred to as follows:—"It is expected by these ultimate arrangements (meaning the end gradients) the locomotive engines in the Great Western Railway will have nowhere to surmount a greater inclination than 5 or 6 feet per mile, and probably even less, the only two inclined planes of 1 in 100, at Box and Wootton Bassett, being worked by stationary power. These very favourable gradients, unequalled in any railway of great extent now in progress, will ensure such an economy in the cost of locomotive power as materially to reduce the estimated annual expenses. They will, moreover, greatly facilitate the attainment of a higher speed of travelling. Under these peculiar circumstances, and with the view of obtaining the full advantage of the regularity and the reduction of power effected by this near approach to a level, and also to remedy several serious inconveniences experienced in existing railways, an increased width of rails has been recommended by your engineer, and, after mature consideration, has been determined upon by the Board. Difficulties and objections were at first supposed by some persons to exist in the construction of engines for this increased width of rails, but the directors have pleasure in stating that several of the most experienced locomotive engine manufacturers in the North have undertaken to construct these, and several are now contracted for, adapted to the peculiar track and dimensions of this railway, calculated for a minimum velocity of 30 miles per hour. These engines will be capable of attaining a rate of 35 or 40 miles per hour, with the same facility as 25 to 30 miles is gained by those now constructed for other lines."

It was thus the great battle of the gauges had its beginning, and these were the rates of the speed to be obtained. As I before said, I liked the gauge and the scope it gave for improving the engines, but the designs of the engines then contracted for were bad. I, however, had made up my mind to do my best to aid Mr. Brunel in carrying out his views. While inspecting these engines, I also bought a number of tools for the repairing shops.

I spent the 24th of August, the day I came of age, with my mother at Warwick, and on my return from the North I went to live at West Drayton, as being a central place between London and Maidenhead. The company provided me with a horse and gig. We also built an engine-house here, supposing that trains would start from West Drayton, and the first piece of the line was finished between the Drayton engine house and the Dogkennel Bridge through the cutting towards Maidenhead. The first engine delivered to the railway was the "Vulcan," built by the Vulcan Foundry Company. She was first in steam on the rail on the 9th January 1838; a second from the same firm, and two from Mather Dixon & Co., followed in a week or so. These came by canal to West Drayton, and I had to get them from there to the engine-house, about a mile off. The "North Star" engine was delivered by barge on the river at Maidenhead in January, and was first in steam on the 15th January 1838. The first running of the engines was celebrated by a dinner at West Drayton on the 16th January. Some Irish gentlemen took more wine than was good for them, and amused themselves by dancing an Irish war dance on our hats, which happened to be piled up in a corner of the room. I was rather disgusted with the termination of our dinner, and resolved never to have anything to do with another. I was one of the stewards. I went to my first London party on the 29th January. It was at Mrs. Horsley's, Mrs. Brunel's mother. I believe I did succeed in getting as far as the staircase, and left it disgusted with London parties, making a note in my memorandum-book never to go to another. I had to drive all the way from West Drayton to get there, and to walk from a public-house, where I put up and got a bed, in silk stockings and thin shoes. I spent my Christmas in the North, chiefly at Mr. Tanner's.

The time had now arrived when I thought myself sufficiently fixed in life to get married. On March 22, 1838, I was married at Bishop Wearmouth church by Mr. Grant to Miss Margaret Tanner. It took place, on account of Mrs. Tanner's state of health, in a very quiet manner. A postchaise (things that have gone out of use) was brought to the back-door of Mr. Tanner's house, and Margaret and I, accompanied by Mr. Temfield, an old friend of Mr. Tanner's, went in it to church. The day was quietly spent at Mr. Tanner's house. I was anxious to get back to the railway, but did not leave Sunderland until Sunday night. We went by a postchaise to Durham, and took the coach early next morning for London, arriving there about five o'clock on the Tuesday afternoon, or in thirty-six hours, a very different time from that now occupied by the same journey. We went on to West Drayton the same night, where I had taken part of a furnished house, and my mother was there to receive us.

I took a good deal of interest at this time in the building of the *Great Western* steamship. She was intended to sail between Bristol and America. She was a design of Mr. Brunel's, and, like many of his ideas, the world would not believe in her. Indeed, Dr. Lardner *proved* that she could not cross the Atlantic. However, on the 31st March 1838 steam was got up in her, and a trial made. All went well with the ship, but Mr. Brunel had a serious accident by falling down one of the hatchways and severely injuring himself. It was a most unfortunate time for him, as every effort was being made to get the railway open. The Great Western steamship made her voyage to America, and has since been a most successful ship. None of her size have done better. She was broken up in 1857.

I was much engaged up to the end of May in getting all ready for opening the portion of the Great Western Railway from London to Maidenhead. On the 31st May the directors made their first trip over the whole length of this portion, and it was opened to the public on the 4th June, and then my difficulties with the engines began. The "North Star" and the six from the Vulcan Foundry Company were the only ones I could at all depend upon. The result was I had to begin in a measure to rebuild one half of the stock I had to work with. For many weeks my nights were spent in a carriage in the engine-house at Paddington, as repairs had to be done to the engines at night to get them to do their work next day. The "North Star" being the most powerful one, and in other respects the best, was my chief reliance, but she was often getting into trouble from other causes. I began to think railway life was a very hard and anxious one. I was soon obliged to leave West Drayton and go to Paddington to live, having taken furnished lodgings in the Harrow Road. When I look back upon that time, it is a marvel to me that we escaped serious accidents. It was no uncommon thing to take an engine out on the line to look for a late train that was expected, and many times have I seen the train coming and reversed the engine, and ran back out of its way as quickly as I could. What would be said of such a mode of proceeding now?

The failure of so many engines made the directors very anxious, and they called upon me, apart from Mr. Brunel, to make them a report on each engine. I had hitherto done all I could to get them into working order, and had reported to Mr. Brunel alone, as my chief; but the directors having called upon me for a separate report, I felt I was placed in a great difficulty, as I could only tell what I believed to be the facts. I, however, had no choice, and had to make this report, in which I condemned the construction of the engines. This alarmed the directors, and obtained for me a rather angry letter from Mr. Brunel. I will, however, do him the justice to say that he only showed it in his letter, and was personally most kind and considerate to me, leaving me to deal with the stock as I thought best. His good sense told him what I said was correct, and his kind heart did me justice. I was shortly after, with his full consent and support, instructed to prepare designs for the future stock, of which it had become necessary to order a large quantity. These drawings I took great pains with, giving every detail much thought and consideration, and the result was designs for two classes of engines,—one with a 7-feet driving wheel, 15-inch cylinder, and 18-inch stroke, and another with 6-feet wheel, 14-inch cylinder, and 18-inch stroke, both with ample boiler power; and I may with confidence, after these engines have been working for twenty-eight years, say that no better engines for their weight have since been constructed either by myself or others. They have done, and continue to do, admirable duty; advantage has been taken of new cylinders being required to give them an extra inch in diameter and 4 inches more in stroke, and expansion gear has been added; in other respects the engines are the same.

When I had completed the drawings, I had them lithographed and specifications printed, and thin iron templates for those parts it was essential should be interchangeable, and these were supplied to the various engine-builders with whom contracts were made. One hundred and forty-two engines were let, and all the makers did their work well. The best were built by Fenton, Murray, & Jackson, of Leeds, but the great durability of the engines has proved that all did their work well. I very frequently visited the various works where they were built. My chief draftsman at that time was also a clever fellow, and he has made a good position for himself since as a contractor. His name is Thomas Crampton (he died April 1888). A drawing now at Clewer[1] of the 7-feet engine was made by him, and shows the design, but I have also a very perfect working model of the engine at my house in London. This model is a beautiful piece of work; many of the parts were made by Clements, who used to be in those days the best workman in London. I also value the drawings very much, and would wish both to be carefully preserved in the family by my eldest son.

No sooner was the Great Western Railway opened than a strong party amongst the shareholders was organised in Lancashire and the North to condemn the broad gauge, and they appointed Mr. Hawkshaw, then an engineer in Manchester, and Mr. Nicholas Wood of Newcastle-on-Tyne to report upon it, for which purpose they required a great many experiments to be made, had instruments for testing the deflection of the road, &c. They appointed Dr. Lardner to conduct the experiments for them, and the Doctor's calculations were little more reliable in the matter of the power and speed of the locomotive than they had been with regard to the *Great Western* steamship crossing the Atlantic. He said the "North Star" engine could only at 45 miles per hour draw a load of 15 tons. I tried her the next day and took 50 tons.

A very elaborate report was made by both these gentlemen, and presented to the shareholders of the Great Western at a meeting held at the London Tavern on the 9th January 1839. Mr. Hawkshaw in his report condemned the whole thing, while Mr. Wood admitted many advantages in the broad gauge.

As the shareholders were entering the meeting, a very clever paper written by Mr. George Clark (who at the time was on the Great Western acting as an engineer—he is now the manager of the Dowlais Iron Works) was put into their hands. This paper turned the dispute into ridicule, and there is no doubt had a good deal of effect on the result. There were 7792 votes for the directors, and 6145 against them, so that, as far as the Great Western shareholders were concerned, the matter was settled by a majority of 1647 votes. This decision the shareholders never attempted to disturb.

I was very much interested in this fight, and had devoted a great deal of time to counteract the conclusions of the narrow-gauge party. A much better result was obtained from the "North Star" before the meeting than was obtained when Dr. Lardner made his experiment. I made some experiments on the blast-pipe by increasing its size, and also taking great care that the steam was discharged up the middle of the chimney, and it was wonderful how much the large size from the cylinders and the care in discharging the steam still enabled us to get plenty of it. The effect and power of the blast-pipe had not before been sufficiently considered in the locomotive. Mr. Brunel had a notion that if the orifice was made in the form of a cross it would be more effective, and he and I worked by ourselves most of Christmas day in the upper smith's shop, constructing a tip of this shape; but nothing succeeded so well as the plain round orifice. We kept our trials on this matter very quiet, intending to spring it as a mine against our opponents after they had committed themselves to their report, and it will be seen, by reference to the report of the directors, that they made good use of it. Mr. Brunel having called upon me for a report upon the question of the gauge, I wrote a very full one, and was glad to get a kind letter from him, saying how much both he and the directors were pleased with it; and some portions of it were included in their report to the shareholders.

Before the end of 1838 I had taken rooms on Paddington Green, and on 1st June 1839 my first child was born there.

The neighbourhood of Paddington at that time was very different from what it has since become. It was then almost impossible to get a house, and lodgings such as would suit me were very scarce. My salary was only £550 per annum; but as I began life with the determination never to spend the whole of my income, be it what it might, or the saving ever so small, if I saved a pound, I was sure I did not get into debt. I advise all young people to do this. It will add, not only to their present peace of mind, but to their future success in life. Nothing is so destructive to the mind as the feeling of being in debt. Illness or misfortune may force it upon you, but apart from these two causes it should be avoided as you would poison.

Little occurred in railway matters during 1839 after the January meeting.

Mr. Brunel had rather an amusing victory over his enemies in the autumn of 1839. Maidenhead Bridge consists chiefly of two flat brick arches of 128 feet span each. They were built in brickwork, and people were pleased to say they would not stand, and a newspaper authority in railway matters used to send a commissioner down every week to report upon it. This he did by describing the cracks, &c. They said, as it was resting on the centres, as soon as Mr. Brunel took them away the bridge must follow. One Friday night there was a great storm of wind and rain, and the centres were blown down during the night. The paper came out on the Saturday morning with statements and opinions rather stronger than usual; but before it was in the hands of the readers the arches were standing alone, and have stood well ever since. They had not been resting on the centering for some time before.

1840.—During this year further portions of the Great Western were opened, and agreements were made for leasing the Bristol and Exeter and the Swindon and Cheltenham Railways, and it became necessary to furnish large works for the repair, &c., of our stock. I was called upon to report on the best situation to build these works, and on full consideration I reported in favour of Swindon, it being the junction with the Cheltenham Branch, and also a convenient division of the Great Western line for the engine-working. Mr. Brunel and I went down to look at the ground, then only green fields, and he agreed with me as to its being the best place. The matter is referred to in the directors' report of February 1841. By this time I was much more comfortable with regard to our engines; the new engines ordered to my drawings were being delivered. The "Firefly," started on March 1840, was the first, and they all gave every one general satisfaction. We could now calculate with some certainty, not only upon the speed they could run, but also upon their not breaking down upon the journey. We had no difficulty in running at sixty miles per hour with good loads. I may mention, as a contrast of the locomotive expenses per mile up to that time as compared with that they have since become, that they were then about 1s. 6d. per mile, and are now between 7d. and 8d. No doubt the cost of fuel was one of the chief sources of saving, and getting a greater mileage out of the engines.

In November of this year 1840 I took out a patent for steeling the surface of rails and tires, either by the mode of cementing the surface after the rails or tires were manufactured, or by welding a slab of steel on the surface of the pile. Careful experiments made at the Haigh Foundry Company's works at Wigan, in Lancashire, showed that the latter mode was the best. Mr. Stubbs, the steel manufacturer of Warrington, assisted us in these experiments, and although we never used it for rail-making on account of the cost, we succeeded in making good sound tires, containing about one-fifth part of best shear steel. The large price paid at that time for steel made the tires costly in first cost, and interfered with their general introduction; but I used them exclusively on our engines and tenders, and the result of their working showed a very large economy in their use. Many of them ran a distance of between 200,000 and 300,000 miles. Latterly, from the great progress that has been made in the cheap manufacture of steel, solid steel tires and rails also have come into very general use; but I am still of opinion that for tires the plan I used of making the surface only of steel is much the best, because they can be hardened, the iron in the tire being depended upon for toughness, while the hard steel formed the wearing surface. A solid steel tire cannot be hardened, as it would be brittle and dangerous; there is therefore, in my opinion, as much difference in the life of the two kinds of tire as there would be between two anvils, one having the face hardened and the other left soft. The extreme hardness of my steel tires made it impossible to turn them in the ordinary manner. I was therefore obliged to design machinery for grinding them. This was done by having on the slide-rest a revolving grindstone a couple of feet in diameter, running at about 1000 revolutions per minute. This the men soon learned to use with as much care as a turner does his cutting tool. The wheels themselves were made to revolve in the opposite direction from the grindstone at the rate of about 200 revolutions per minute. Great truth was obtained in the wheels, and a very good job made of them at very little additional cost beyond turning the iron tires. This patent did not pay me during the whole of its time more than between £5000 and £6000, and I found so much trouble connected with it and the false position I felt placed in with our own Company, that I never took out another, nor do I ever approve of engineers who have to advise large Companies being themselves interested in patents. I look upon the patent law as a great curse to this country. It cannot be worked with perfect honesty. Patents are taken out for all kinds of absurd things, and by people with little or no practical knowledge of the work they undertake, and the really practical man in carrying out his work is met at all points by the claims of some patentee. I have in my practice constantly found the disadvantage of the law; not that I object to reward a man for a real invention; but the real inventors are rare, while the patents are counted by thousands. The absence of a patent law would not retard invention. The human mind will scheme and study for the pleasure of the work, and the honour of being the originator of a real improvement would be a sufficient stimulus. I have no doubt the day is not far distant when some important modification of the patent law will be made. The existing law is a great improvement on the old one, when a man was not obliged to disclose his invention at the time of securing his patent. It was a common practice for a man to patent a general title, and then wait his six months to see what ideas of other people be picked up to put in his description.

1841.—The whole of the Great Western Railway between London and Bristol was opened on the 30th June 1841. The question of working through the Box tunnel up a gradient of 1 in 100 was a source of much anxiety to Mr. Brunel. We had found all difficulties at the Wootton Bassett incline disappear, but it was much shorter than Box, and was also not a tunnel. I cannot say I felt any anxiety, as I had seen how well our engines took their load up Wootton Bassett without the help of a bank-engine, and with the assistance of a bank-engine at Box, I felt we would have no difficulty. Only one line of rails was complete through the tunnel the day we opened, and the trains had therefore to be worked on a single line. I undertook to accompany all the trains through the tunnel, and did so the first day and night, also the second day, intending to be relieved when the mail came down on the second night. At about eleven o'clock that night we had a very narrow escape from a fearful accident. I was going up the tunnel with the last up-train, when I fancied I saw some green lights placed as they were in front of our trains. A second's reflection convinced me it was the mail coming down. I lost no time in reversing the engine I was on and running back to Box Station with my train as quickly as I could, when the mail came down behind me. The policeman at the top of the tunnel had made some blunder and sent the mails on when they arrived there. Had the tunnel not been pretty clear of steam, we must have met in full career, and the smash would have been fearful, cutting short my career also. But, as though mishaps never came alone, when I was taking my train up again, from some cause or other the engine got off the rails in the tunnel, and I was detained there all night before I got all straight again. I need not say I was not sorry to get home and to bed at Paddington, after two days and nights' pretty hard work. Mr. Brunel was at the time living in Bath, and he was very kind to me in sending me plenty of good food, &c., to keep my steam up. Box tunnel had a very pretty effect for the couple of days it was worked as a single line, from the number of candles used by the men working on the unfinished line; it was a perfect illumination, extending through the whole tunnel, nearly two miles long.

I made at this time a number of experiments on the use of peat as a fuel. Lord Willoughby D'Eresby took a great interest in the matter, and we tried it in various ways, some caked and some merely compressed very hard. We were able to keep steam with it, but the consumption was very large, certainly four times that of ordinary coke made from coal; it would therefore require a very large difference in the value per ton to render such a fuel profitable.

On Tuesday, the 24th August 1841, I went to the House of Lords to hear the Queen read her Speech, and stayed there in the evening, when I had an opportunity of hearing the Duke of Wellington speak. He moved an amendment to the address, and I was much struck with the methodical manner in which he referred to his papers. He had a packet of them in his hand and referred to them in turn, but always putting the paper away in its proper place in the packet when done with. Lord Melbourne was then Prime Minister, and answered him. The result was the Government was beaten and went out of office. It was the only time I ever heard the great Duke speak.

My son Henry was born on the 30th December 1841.

The Queen had given up travelling between London and Windsor by road, and had gone by us. While I held the office of locomotive engineer on the Great Western, I nearly in all cases took charge of the engine myself when the Queen travelled, and have been so fortunate as never to have a single delay with her, and she has travelled under my care a great many miles. I was the first who had such a charge, and it was some time before she had occasion to travel on any line but the Great Western.

We started the machinery at the Swindon works on the 28th November 1842. Archie Sturrock was our local manager, but the works were not put into regular operation until Monday, the 2nd January 1843.

1843.—During this year further portions of the Great Western Railway branches and the Bristol and Exeter were opened. The *Great Britain* steamship, one of those large ideas of Mr. Brunel's, was launched at Bristol. She was then considered a monster ship, although now she is a very ordinary one, and every one blamed Mr. Brunel for building anything so large.

I took Prince Albert down by special train to the launch on the 19th July 1843. It was a lovely day and the sight a beautiful one. As the ship was built in a dry dock, the launch only consisted in floating her out. On the down journey we had some long stops for the Prince to receive addresses, but having no delays on the return journey, it was done in two hours four minutes. Few runs over so long a distance have been made as quick as this, even since.

1844.—On the 1st of May in this year the railway was opened throughout to Exeter. We had a special train with a large party from London to go down to the opening. A great dinner was given in the goods shed at Exeter Station. I worked the train with the "Actaeon" engine, one of our 7-feet class, with six carriages. We left London at 7.30 A.M. and arrived at Exeter at 12.30, having had some detention over the hour fixed. On the return journey we left Exeter at 5.20 P.M., and stopped at Paddington platform at ten. Sir Thomas Acland, who was with us, went at once to the House of Commons, and by 10.30 got up and told the House he had been in Exeter at 5.20, the distance 195 miles. It was a very hard day's work for me, as, apart from driving the engine a distance of 390 miles, I had to be out early in the morning to see that all was right for our trip, and while at Exeter was busy with matters connected with the opening, so that my only chance of sitting down was for the hour we were at dinner. Next day my back ached so much I could hardly walk. Mr. Brunel wrote me a very handsome letter, thanking me for what I had done, and all were very much pleased.

The question of the gauge of railways was beginning again to become an important question to us. As the extension of lines took place, it became a fight between the broad gauge companies and the narrow gauge companies as to who should get possession of the various adjoining districts, we contending that, as the broad gauge was best, we ought to be encouraged, and, as will be seen, for the next few years my time and thoughts were nearly entirely directed to this fight. From what I saw on the occasion of this trip to Exeter, I felt we might safely put on a regular train that would perform the distance between London and Exeter in four and a half hours, and advised the directors to do so as an express train at higher fares. This was shortly after done, and was the beginning of that important system of express trains which has given so much comfort and accommodation to the public. I may therefore, I think, claim to be the father of express trains.

During the year 1844 I tried the experiment of using corrugated copper fire-boxes on an engine, thinking by that means I would greatly enlarge the heating surface. Experience showed me that perhaps a little more reflection might have told me beforehand that it did no good; the temperature of the gases escaping from the chimney was not higher than it ought to be, and therefore as all the heat given out by the fire was already taken up, I did not obtain any benefit, as I did not increase the bulk of the fire. It made a strong box, but was a very costly one, and I only put it to two engines.

Louis Philippe, King of the French, was at Windsor in October 1844, and travelled on our line.

On the 11th of December the *Great Britain* steamship was ready for trial, and I went down to Bristol to go out to sea with her. When she entered the lock leading into the river, she caught the copings on each side and could not get through. Fortunately, they were very quick in hauling her back, or she would have been a fixture, and have probably been a wreck. She was, however, got free and back into the dock, and the lock walls were lowered and we got out the next tide, and the following day went into the Channel with her, where she performed admirably. She soon after began her voyages to America from Liverpool, and after a few voyages was run aground in Dundrum Bay, on the coast of Ireland, where she lay a whole winter exposed to the action of the sea, but stood it well, and was then got off. She was a heavy loss to the shareholders, as she was then sold to Messrs. Gibbs of Liverpool for a very small sum. They took her engines out and made sundry changes in her, and she has since been employed profitably in the Australian trade. The engines, as constructed originally, drove the screw by a pitch chain from a large wheel worked by the engines to a smaller one on the screw shaft. I think the proportions were about 3 to 1. Although at the time of her first going to sea she was considered too large for any trade or port, she is now a very ordinary-sized ship. I think her tonnage is about 3500.

1845.—This year began our hardest gauge fight. The Great Western went to Parliament for a line from Oxford through Worcester to Wolverhampton, then known as the Oxford, Worcester, and Wolverhampton line. This was to be on the broad gauge, and it was strongly opposed by the London and Birmingham Company. I had to give evidence on the bill, and had prepared very elaborate tables showing the speed and economy of the broad gauge. The Committee of the House of Commons sat on it rather over three weeks, and gave us the bill on the 4th June. We met in a temporary committee-room, and the crowd and heat was excessive. Sitting in this heat all day, and working most of the night in preparing evidence for the witnesses, almost broke me down. I will never forget the passion George Stephenson got into when the decision of the Committee was announced. He gave me his mind very freely for fighting the broad gauge against the narrow, in which he said I had been reared. I was not only fighting for my convictions, but also for my employers, who expressed themselves well satisfied with what I had done. The London and North-Western and Grand Junction started express trains to Liverpool on the 1st of May during this fight. I went by the first ones, so as to be able to make use in my evidence of any facts I could pick up. When the bill was reported to the House, the narrow gauge interests moved a resolution on the 20th June, as follows:—"That a humble address be presented to Her Majesty to give a Commission to inquire whether, in all future Acts for the construction of railways, provision ought to be made for securing an uniform gauge, and whether it would be practicable and expedient to bring existing lines of railway in Great Britain, and lines now in course of construction, into uniform gauge, and if so, to report on the best mode of carrying these objects into effect in the present session of Parliament."

The motion was lost by a majority of 2 to 1, and our bill passed. The bill also got passed safely through the Lords without very much difficulty. It was afterwards moved by Mr. Cobden in the House of Commons that a Commission should be appointed in pretty much the words of the former resolution, which was carried unopposed.

The commissioners appointed were Sir F. Smith, R.E.; Professor Airy, the Astronomer Royal; and Professor P. Barlow.

When it is considered that the fight was to be between one railway company on the broad gauge and the host of narrow-gauge companies, it would have been well to put some more practical men on the Commission. For one witness we could call, the narrow-gauge interests could call a dozen. Mr. R. Stephenson, Mr. Locke, and Mr. Bidder were the three engineers of highest standing who were opposed to us.

The commissioners met for the first time on the 6th August 1845. After the Parliamentary fight was over, Mr. Brunel and Mr. Saunders, Secretary and General Manager of the Great Western Railway, went abroad, and the question before the commissioners was left to me alone, a responsibility I did not much like; but it was to be, so I undertook the task. Mr. R. Stephenson was the first witness called; he was followed by Mr. Locke and a host of others, officers and engineers of narrow-gauge lines. The general principles laid down by them against the broad gauge were:—First, that the engines were too large and heavy, and the large wheels used were not necessary, as the small wheels and engines of the narrow-gauge companies were able to run at as high speeds as it was safe for the public to work the trains; second, that the broad-gauge carriages were too large—the public did not like to sit four abreast; third, that the cost of working was greater. A reference to the detailed evidence in the blue book will show that these were the chief points attempted to be made by the narrow-gauge companies. I may also say the question of the disadvantage of break of gauge was dwelt upon. I gave my evidence on the 17th and 21st of October, putting in a number of tables and calculations to disprove the above assertions, and to show that the broad gauge could carry traffic at a higher speed and at a less cost than the narrow gauge. Mr. Brunel and Mr. Saunders were examined on their return from the Continent at the end of November. As it was clear the commissioners were unable to make up their minds upon the question from the contradiction of the two opposing factions, we prepared to bring the matter to a practical test by direct experiment, and proposed that we should each work trains of various weights over long lengths of railway to test the speed as well as cost. The narrow-gauge parties made great objections to this, although they had been getting new engines built of larger dimensions (but very faulty in construction) for the purpose of trying to work their express trains at our speed. They constructed the boilers of great length, without getting any more heating surface in the fire-box, and allowed this exceptional length to overhang the wheels at each end. The "White Horse of Kent," on which I had a number of experiments made, was so unsteady that it was necessary to be tied on to make experiments on the smoke-box temperature, and the tube surface was carried to so great an extent, that the heat in the smoke-box was less than the temperature of the steam used, so that one end of the engine was actually acting as a condenser. After much trouble, however, it was at last settled to make experiments; but not, as we proposed them, over a long length of railway, as from London to Bristol and back, as against London to Birmingham and back, where there would be a variation in the gradients, and the engine would be required, as in ordinary work, to take in cold water on the road; but it must be on a piece of short local line, and the narrow-gauge parties selected the piece between York and Darlington, a practical level also, against about the same length of our line out of London, or 46 miles. Experiments were to be made with trains of 50, 60, 70, and 80 tons passenger, and 200 and 400 tons with goods. We made our experiments with our old engines, having no new ones built for the purpose; the "Ixion" was used for the passenger work, and the "Sampson" for the goods. Our experiments were gone through on the days and at the hours fixed, and we were unfortunate on two of the days in having a high wind on one, and a small drizzling rain on the other, making us slip. When it came to the time of the 50-ton train, the narrow-gauge party would not have it worked, saying after the result of the others it was unnecessary.

[*The performances of the narrow-gauge trains are narrated in a graphic manner in a passage here omitted.*]

We all returned to London on the 3rd January 1846 to make our reports, and the commissioners were allowed to prepare their report upon such data as they had got. The conclusion they arrived at was that the narrow gauge should be the national gauge; but, in referring to the experiments, they said, "That we consider them as confirmatory of the statement and results given by Mr. Gooch in his evidence, proving as they do that the broad gauge engines possess greater capabilities for speed with equal loads, and, generally speaking, of propelling greater loads with equal speed, and, moreover, that the working of such engines is economical when very high speeds are required, or when the load to be conveyed requires the full power of the engine." It was a hard fight, and there is no doubt, so far as the evil of break of gauge was concerned, we had a weak case, although everything possible was done to strengthen it. A machine was constructed at Paddington by which loads could be easily transferred from one gauge to another, by changing the body of waggon, load and all, or by lifting the narrow-gauge waggons complete upon a broad gauge platform. We also schemed a waggon with telescope axles, adapted to run on either gauge, but I never had any faith in any of these plans as workable in practice. A break of gauge meant the unloading one set of waggons and putting the goods into another. This has since been done in practice with a platform between the two lines of waggons. The cost of this, apart from delay, is about threepence per ton on an average, and this may be taken as the maximum of the cost. The other points contended for by the narrow gauge during this fight they have since in practice given up; for they now make their engines quite as heavy as the broad gauge; their carriages are also as heavy, and they put four people abreast, and they do run high speeds with express trains, without any particular danger to the public.

While the Commission was sitting, I went to France and Belgium in September for ten days, to see the plan adopted by the French for transfixing the body of the diligences upon railway trucks.

A very carefully prepared answer to the commissioners' report was prepared by Mr. Brunel, Mr. Saunders, and myself. We had some good fun over it. We met at Mr. Saunders' house for a few hours each day until it was complete, and we of course proved that the commissioners had come to quite a wrong conclusion, as will be seen in the printed papers or blue book, to which I refer those who take an interest in the question for all the details.

1846—On the 15th January the directors of the Great Western sent for me to the board-room, and Mr. Russell, after very kindly speaking of what I had done in the gauge fight, presented me with a cheque for £500, and increased my salary by £300 a year. When I first joined the Great Western, it was fixed at £300, but when the line opened it was increased to £550, and in January 1841 to £700. The increase now made it £1000. It was raised on the 1st January 1851 to £1500, at which it stood until I left the service.

The experiments and results of the gauge contest before the commissioners induced us to build some larger engines, and I prepared one with 18-inch cylinders, 2-feet stroke, and 8-feet wheels. This engine was ordered by the Board, and, as it was important to get it to work before the next session of Parliament, when a renewal of the fight would take place, I arranged for night and day work upon her, and had her finished in thirteen weeks from the day of getting the order, probably as quick a job as was ever done. She was first tried at the end of April 1846, and on the 13th June we made a sensational trip with her to Bristol with a load of 100 tons. Mr. Russell, and the directors, and Mr. Brunel went down; a dinner was given to a large party at Bristol, and a good deal of speech-making took place. We attained a steady speed of 62 miles per hour with this load. The distance to Swindon was done in one hour eighteen minutes, and to Bristol in two hours twelve minutes, including stoppages. Mr. Russell called this a "great fact," and it was a great fact. Had we had this engine ready in time for the gauge experiments, how different would the results have been, although I don't suppose it would have altered the report. We called the engine the "Great Britain;" she was built on six wheels, but finding the weight too much on the leading wheels, I put another pair forward.

My third son, Alfred, was born on the 2nd March of this year, 1846.

1847.—The passing of the direct line from Oxford to Birmingham again raised the question of gauge, as the Gauge Act, passed on the recommendation of the Gauge Commission, required that all future lines should be made on the narrow gauge, without Parliament's sanction to its being broad; and the House of Lords on the 25th June 1847 ordered an inquiry by the Railway Commissioners of the Board of Trade as to the accommodation of the lines between London and Birmingham, and whether it is expedient to lay the broad gauge to Birmingham, &c., such report to be made to the next session of Parliament.

The Railway Commissioners, in carrying out these instructions (these were not the *Gauge* Commissioners, but

the Board of Trade), sent out a series of printed questions
to the London and North-Western Company and the Great
Western. These questions referred chiefly to the resistance of
railway trains and construction of locomotives. On the part
of the London and North-Western a joint answer was given
by Mr. R. Stephenson, Mr. Locke, Mr. M'Connell, and Mr.
Trevithick, the two latter gentlemen being the locomotive
superintendents of the London and North Western
Company. Mr. Brunel sent in his answer, and I sent in mine
separately, on behalf of the Great Western. To enable me to
do this satisfactorily, I felt a complete series of experiments
was required, and having the authority of the Board to spend
what was necessary, I designed and constructed an indicator
to measure and accurately record the speed the train was
moving, and also on the same paper to record the traction
power used by the engine measured by a spring, also on the
same paper the force and direction of the wind. To check the
traction I also at the same time took indicator cards from the
cylinder of the engine so as accurately to measure the power
exerted there. It also gave me the power expended in moving
the engines. I made a great number of experiments over a
level piece of line on the Bristol and Exeter line, at various
rates of speed and loads. They gave me results very different
from those obtained by the narrow gauge, which, however,
were done more by calculation than by actual experiment.
I read a paper at the Institution of Civil Engineers on these
experiments in April 1848, and a good deal of discussion
took place on them for a couple of nights. I still keep the
original records of these experiments. They cost me a vast
amount of labour, both in calculations and in making the
experiments. It was rather a difficult task to sit on the buffer
beam of the engine, and take indicator cards at speeds of 60
miles per hour.

Mr. Stephenson endeavoured to show before the Board of Trade that it would be dangerous to have a mixed gauge, that is, three lines of rails, and produced some plans to show the number of points and crossings. Many years' experience has since proved him wrong. The report of the commissioners was in, favour of extending the broad gauge to Birmingham, and making it a mixed gauge line. This was the last of the real gauge fights. Nothing has since transpired to raise the point again, and it may be said from all the evidence and reports, that a difference in the gauge of the railways in this country, now they have so covered its surface, and so large an interchange of traffic has to take place, is an evil, and is now to be regretted, but that, were the whole question now open to be decided, the broad gauge is safer, cheaper, more comfortable, and attains a much higher speed than the narrow, and would be the best for the national gauge. But as the proportion of broad to narrow is so small, there is no doubt the country must submit to a gradual displacement of the broad, and the day will come when it will cease. The fight has been of great benefit to the public; it has pricked on all parties to exertion; the competition of the gauges has introduced high speeds and great improvements in the engines, and was of great practical use to all those who were actively mixed up in the contest, as they were forced to think and experiment. It was not allowed to them to rest quietly on speeds of twenty to thirty miles per hour. I know it was of great value to me by the practical information I obtained in investigations.

The South Devon line was opened in July this year, 1847, between Newton and Totness, over gradients of 1 in 42. I never saw Mr. Brunel so anxious about anything as he was about this opening. Relying upon the Atmospheric principle,[2] he had made these steep inclines, and he feared there might be difficulties in working them. These difficulties disappeared with the day of opening. All our trains went through very well, and at night it seemed a great relief to Mr. Brunel to find it was so. He shook hands with me and thanked me in a very kind manner for my share in the day's work. He never forgot those who helped him in a difficulty.

During the latter part of 1846 and this year, 1847, I had been building my present house in Warwick Road, Paddington, and got it finished, so that I could get into it at the end of September, which I did. My youngest boy, Frank, was born in the old house on the 20th July 1847.

Up to this time I had looked upon the Great Western as an employment for life, and had refused a good offer from Mr. Locke in 1842 to go to the Grand Junction, and also from Alderman Thompson to go to Italy, both at much higher salaries than I was getting; but I felt that a rolling stone gathers no moss, and was unwilling to leave a service in which I was comfortable and well treated. But now I felt it was not safe to rely upon the permanency of such a state of things, and I therefore determined to make myself in some degree independent of the railway, and for this purpose saw the chairman, Mr. Russell, and obtained his consent to my doing any other work, so long as I did not neglect the Great Western. Acting on this principle, I found no difficulty in making money by professional services in other ways, and it is thus what fortune I have realised has been obtained.

I was made a Freemason on the 14th of February 1850 by Mr. Luxmore in the St. George's Lodge, Exeter. Many ridicule the Society of Freemasons, saying there is no secret, and the only object is good dinners. Writing now eighteen years after I was made, and during which time I took a very active part, passing the chair of several lodges, and getting high rank in the craft, being now Deputy Grand Master of Wilts, I look back on my connection with Masonry as a very useful and a very pleasant part of my life. I have made many kind friends in the craft, and have met with much kindness, and have never regretted the day I was initiated into its mysteries.

1851.—This year is chiefly remarkable for the first of those great Exhibitions that have since become rather common. The one held in Hyde Park this year was a charming building, and being the first of the kind, the impression made upon the mind was stronger than with the following ones. The Great Western Company sent a locomotive, the "Lord of the Isles," one of our large class of passenger engines, and I am safe in saying she was a beautiful job, and has ever since done her work on the line satisfactorily.

1856.—In the early part of this year I formed the Ruabon Coal Company. The circumstances were these. It had been found impossible to get a regular coal trade on our line, and I proposed to my company to have some collieries of their own, and went to Wrexham to look at those belonging to Mr. Henry Robertson, and also some property of Sir Watkin W. Wynn's, where a colliery might be sunk. Having obtained the best information I could, I advised the directors to buy up Robertson's works, as they were in operation, and could be made available for our purpose at once. This was finally agreed upon by the directors, and the price settled, but at this time a decision in regard to a similar plan in operation on the Eastern Counties Railway showed it not to be within the powers of the Company, and stopped our plan. Mr. Walpole, our chairman, then asked me if I could find private parties to form a company, and enter into an agreement with the Great Western Company to send a large fixed quantity of coal over their line. This I agreed to do, and took a large stake in the

coal company myself, and was to be the chairman. Feeling
that this might conflict with my position as an officer of the
railway company, I placed my resignation in the hands of
Mr. Walpole; but he and the directors did not think it right
to accept it. I, however, left it in their hands to accept at
any time, should circumstances make it desirable. I felt there
were interests in the coal trade amongst the shareholders of
the railway, who would no doubt object to what had been
done; and such proved to be the case. For two or three half-
years afterwards it was the cause of a row at our meetings, and
some parties went to the Court of Chancery to put an end to
the agreement. In this they failed, and the Court expressed
themselves strongly that what had been done was perfectly
legal and right. I thus got a great deal of abuse by trying to
do a good turn to the shareholders of the railway, and risking
a good deal of money in doing so. The colliery has, however,
been a very good investment, and has done good to both
parties to the arrangement. Mr. Walpole acted very well to
me in this matter, as he never flinched from what he had
told me, but did his best to carry out the arrangement, and
support those who had gone into it at his request.

1859.—In the March of this year I bought Clewer Park, or
rather bought the lease of it from Mrs. Ashley, and afterwards
purchased the freehold from Dr. Proctor. I had been long
looking out for a house in the neighbourhood of Windsor. I
had spent my summer at Windsor for five or six years before,
taking lodgings, and I was very fortunate to get a place so
suitable for me in every respect as Clewer. When I went
down to look at it, a large bed of violets took my fancy very
much, and I saw that the timber, &c., was very fine, and that
the faults I saw in the grounds might be easily remedied. I
therefore had no difficulty in making up my mind to take it.

On the 15th September 1859 I lost my oldest and best friend in the death of Mr. Brunel. He had been far from well for two or three years past, and during that time had been much worried by the *Great Eastern* steamship. This was his last great work; not satisfied with the size of the *Great Britain*, he conceived and designed this noble ship. By his death the greatest of England's engineers was lost, the man of the greatest originality of thought and power of execution, bold in his plans, but right. The commercial world thought him extravagant, but although he was so, great things are not done by those who sit down and count the cost of every thought and act. He was a true and sincere friend, a man of the highest honour, and his loss was deeply deplored by all who had the pleasure to know him. He had a curious accident many years before his death. Playing with a child, he managed to swallow a half sovereign, which went into his chest, and many attempts were made to get it out, without success. He himself suggested the plan which succeeded. He had a frame made swinging like a looking-glass on the centre, to which he was fastened, and then suddenly turned with his head downwards. They failed at first to get it out, but another attempt succeeded, and it was a great joy to his medical men and all with him to see it fall on the floor.

I shall ever feel a deep sense of gratitude to Mr. Brunel for all his kindness and support, from the day I first saw him in 1837.

1. Sir Daniel Gooch's country-house.
2. An account of the trial of the Atmospheric System on the South Devon Railway will be found at pp. 131–170 of the "Life of I.K. Brunel" (London, 1870).

III

THE "GREAT EASTERN" STEAMSHIP AND THE ATLANTIC CABLE-LAYING EXPEDITION OF 1865

1860.—The shareholders of the *Great Eastern* steamship, being out of humour with their directors, at the meeting in February determined to turn them all out and elect a new board. I was requested to form one of the new board, and was elected. After our election we determined to complete the ship fit for sea, and send her a voyage to America as early as we could. I went down to Southampton and took the direction of all the engineering department of the ship. Very many alterations and additions were required both in the general fittings and machinery, the Board of Trade requirements being very large. We raised £100,000 by debentures, and worked hard to get her ready to sail in June. The former captain of the ship, who had been looking after her building (Captain Harrison), was drowned early in the year in Southampton Water, and we had to appoint a new man. We selected Captain Hall. All was sufficiently

The "Great Eastern" steamship, in the gridiron at Milford

complete for us to take our departure in June. I had settled to go with her and take my wife and Harry. We joined the ship at Southampton on Thursday the 14th June. We sailed on the Sunday morning with about twenty passengers, so that we had plenty of room. Two of the other directors went with me, Mr. Barber and Captain Carnegie. All went on most comfortably on our voyage, the weather was very fine, and the ship as steady as an island, so much so that the game of skittles was played every day. One of the passengers, oddly enough, took some skittles on board with him, and assumed the name of Skittles; a sister he had with him also went by the name of Miss Skittles. We had one sharp gale on the passage, lasting a great part of one night, making the ship roll a little. Our general run per day was about 330 knots. We arrived off Sandy Hook very early in the morning of the 28th June, and came to anchor to wait the tide. By ten o'clock craft of all kinds began to arrive from New York to look at us, and our agents came off to us. The scene soon became very exciting, and the day was a lovely one. When we began to run up to New York, we were accompanied by hundreds of yachts, steamers, &c., and it was certainly a grand and exciting scene. As we passed up through that beautiful entrance to the Hudson, the banks were lined with thousands of people, and the forts and American men-of-war saluted us as we passed, so that it was one continual firing of guns and shouting of thousands of people all the way up to New York, and when we came close to that town the scene was wonderful. The wharfs, house-tops, church towers, and every spot where a human being could stand and get a sight of the ship, were crowded. We reached the wharf where we were to lie about five o'clock, and I was very glad when it was time for bed. I did not go ashore. It had been a really hard day's work. I will, however, never forget the beauty of the scene. I now had to undertake a new kind of life—that was to become a showman, as we expected to earn a very large sum of money by exhibiting the ship. We therefore had to advertise and organise our plans, and I cannot say, now it is all over, that we were very clever at our work.

One curious thing happened while we were at New York. A man was to be hanged on Staten Island, which is situated down the harbour. He was taken from New York in a steamer, and the man in office invited a party of his friends to accompany him, providing them with ample refreshments on board, and by way of giving greater pleasure they steamed up the Hudson to the *Great Eastern* to look at her, instead of taking the poor wretch they were about to hang direct to his doom.

On my return to New York, we settled to carry out a pleasure trip with the big ship for two days, that is, we left New York on the Monday afternoon for Cape May, the mouth of the Delaware, spent the next day there, and returned the following night. We started with about 1500 excursionists, and a most extraordinary trip we had. The first night there was no end of fun, and, as the moon was very bright and weather warm, it did very well; but as the passengers had no beds to go to, they lay about anywhere, and in the morning woke up very cross, particularly the reporters to the press, who thought they ought to have been supplied with comfortable cabins, &c., &c. An indignation meeting was held by them, and they went ashore, not to return. The second night we did much better without them, but the newspapers were full of abuse. Most of those who went the trip enjoyed it very much, and passed resolutions accordingly, but on the whole this trip was not a success, and did not pay us, and I was very glad when it was over. One thing I was glad to hear. On the first night a proposal was made, having reference to Mr. Brunel as the designer of the ship, and some hearty cheers given in his honour. We had settled to take the ship to the Chesapeake for a week, and as soon as we returned to New York from Cape May we prepared to start, and sailed from New York on the 2nd August with about a hundred passengers. We had none of the indignant press gentlemen, and had therefore a very pleasant voyage. We reached Point Comfort early the next morning, and spent that day and night there. Thousands of people crowded the little village to see the ship. I went over the large fort here, and had also an opportunity of seeing a number of slaves, who were brought by their masters to see the ship. The kindest and most friendly feeling seemed to exist amongst them, and I have never seen more happiness expressed in the face and manner of the working classes than appeared in these slaves. We left Point Comfort on the morning of the 5th August for Annapolis Roads in the Chesapeake, and had a beautiful sail all day. I was much amused at the disgust of the owners of one of the fast steamers. He had invited a large party to accompany him in the famous steamer, to meet us thirty or forty miles down the bay, and his programme was, he would steam round us and return ahead of us to Annapolis to be ready to receive us. When he met us he certainly turned round, but did not succeed in keeping up with us, and when we cast anchor we could just see his smoke in the distance. Our ship certainly went along nobly. We had it dreadfully hot while we lay here, and thousands of people came from Baltimore and other places to visit the ship. The President visited us on the 9th. He lunched on board, and had a large party of his Cabinet with him. I had a long chat with him on American trade, as it was proposed to us to sail the ship between England and the South with cotton. The President thought well of the scheme. While here I went to Baltimore. It is a large and well-built town. I returned by railway from Baltimore to New York on the 10th August, to get matters completed there to enable us to sail for England on the 16th from New York. We had settled to call at Halifax, at the urgent request of the people there, so that they might see the ship, and our run from New York was the quickest on record. We reached Halifax on the evening of the 18th August, and here we met with a little sharp practice, for although we thus went out of our way to please them, they charged us £350 for light dues, and, although we appealed to the Governor, we failed to get it remitted. This was not much encouragement for us to stop in the place, so we determined to start next morning and let the people see the ship in England if they liked. We worked all night putting our paddle floats out as far as we could, as the ship would be very light before we reached England. The harbour of Halifax is a very fine one, with very deep water up to the edge of the quay. Our ship went within a very few yards of the quay wall.

We got up our anchor at nine in the morning of Sunday the 19th, and started direct for Milford Haven. We had a very pleasant run home, reaching Cape Clear on Sunday the 26th at 4 A.M., and we dropped our anchor at Milford at 4 P.M. It was a very grand sight as we steamed up Milford Haven. The Channel Fleet, consisting of eleven or twelve ships, was lying up the harbour in line, and, as we passed them, each ship manned her yards and gave us hearty cheers, a happy welcome to our home. A special train was waiting to take us to London, but no one wanted to leave the ship that day, and our departure was postponed until the following morning, amid the cheers of the passengers. It is not often passengers wish to sleep another night on board ship after a voyage; but such was the comfort of the *Great Eastern* that all felt regret that it was time to leave her.

The result of our voyage, although perfectly satisfactory as proving the speed and comfort of the ship, was not a profitable one. We carried very few passengers in either direction and no goods, and the heavy expenses in America used up all the money we took for exhibiting her. Although this was our first voyage, yet we were not stopped one moment on account of any defect in the machinery. I was glad I had accompanied her, although I will not again undertake the duties of a showman either of big ships or anything else.

The *Great Eastern* was laid up at Milford for the winter, and put on the gridiron there. A good deal was done to her.

1861.—We had been hard at work on the *Great Eastern* all the winter at Milford, getting her ready for another trip to America. We had some difficulty in getting her off the gridiron. It was an awfully wet and rough night, and, by some blundering of the pilot, her anchors were not let go in time, and she went into a man-of-war, doing her damage to the extent of £350, which we had afterwards to pay. She sailed in May and made a good voyage, returning to Liverpool. She had about 7000 tons of cargo on her return trip, chiefly corn, and the earnings of the voyage more than covered the expenses.[1] We sent her away again from Liverpool with a good lot of passengers in September. We were in capital spirits about her, and I arranged, after she sailed, to go to Mr. Baker's house near Worcester, who was at the time chairman of the Ship Company, to talk over our future, believing a bright one was in store for us. I went there, and we had just finished dinner, and were preparing to close in near a comfortable fire and have our chat, when the servant came in with a telegram saying the ship was off the Irish coast. This spoilt our wine and our hopes, and, instead of discussing her future, we had to speculate upon the cause of her return. Of course this led us to no result, and we went to bed hoping to hear more the following day. I had not been very long asleep, when a knock at my door awoke me, and poor Baker walked into my room with a fresh telegram in his hand. I will never forget his appearance as he stood at the foot of my bed to read the telegram, wrapped up in a white flannel dressing-gown, and one of the old-fashioned night-caps on his head, a lamp in one hand, and the telegram in the other. This telegram did not give us more information; so I went to sleep again, but in a short time another telegram arrived, and a similar scene was gone through. Next day we had full particulars, the ship had got into a heavy gale and her rudder-head had broken, and she was left for a couple of days to the mercy of the wind and sea, until a temporary arrangement could be made to steer her. She had a very bad time of it, but got safely into Queenstown. Both her paddles were carried away. We got her over to Milford again, and put her on the gridiron for repairs. These repairs were very costly, and cleared away much more than our profits. We, however, set about the work, and during the winter got her all ready again for sea.

We started the new rail mill at Swindon in May 1861. I had advised our directors to make their own rails, and, at a cost of £25,000, put up a very good mill.

I now began to think of retiring from the Great Western. I had ample income independent of them, and, in my own mind, settled to give up at the end of twenty-five years' service, which would end in August 1862. I was further inclined to this by the prospect of an amalgamation taking place between the three companies, viz., the Great Western, the South Wales, and the West Midland.

1862.—I was a good deal engaged this year in designing and building engines to work the Metropolitan Underground Railway, as our company had agreed to work it. Some years ago I tried some experiments as to the distance an engine would work without having any blast upon her fire, with a view of making such a line of railway, where it would not do to have the gases, &c., from the chimney discharged into the tunnel. I simply made an ordinary engine, but fitted it with tanks under the boiler, into which I discharged the waste steam by reversing a valve at the bottom of the blast-pipe, so that when the engine was in open cutting, she worked like any other engine, but when in the tunnel the blast was stopped, and a good ash-pan damper destroyed the blast. This engine I found answered very well, and has been the one used. Many suggestions were made. One was to fill the fire-box with red-hot bricks at the end of each trip; but such schemes never would have been practicable.

Our big ship made three voyages to New York this year, each time increasing the number of her passengers. The last voyage, in August, she carried 1530 out, but unfortunately, as she was entering Long Island Sound, she touched upon some rocks and did a great deal of damage to her outer skin, one hole being 80 feet long by about 10 feet wide, with three other holes of less size. So little was this felt on board that none of the passengers had any knowledge of it until they got up in the morning at New York, and then only from a list she had got from the water between the skins on that side. This was a most unfortunate accident for us, and I fear, to some extent, a careless one. It was a fine moonlight night when she struck, and she was at the time slowing speed to take the pilot on board. The excuse made was that these rocks were not shown in the chart. This accident detained the ship in New York for repairs until the early part of 1863. The work was very well managed without putting her on a gridiron, but lost us about £70,000, and pretty well ruined us.

1863.—On the 30th June the *Great Eastern* sailed again for New York with a very large number of passengers, and I went with her as far as Queenstown; but our funds had got so low, that on her return from this trip we were obliged to lay her up, and the bondholders took possession of her, all the original capital having been lost. The two accidents cost us not less than £130,000.

1864.—In the commencement of this year a great effort was being made to make another attempt to lay an Atlantic cable. The Atlantic Company could not find the money, and it was suggested to form a strong company who would purchase Glass & Elliott's works, and also the Gutta-percha Works, and, by a good command of capital, be able to undertake the contract with a large payment in shares and bonds. I was asked to join this combination, and become a director. This I did, taking £20,000 in shares. Mr. Pender of Manchester was elected chairman, and we had no difficulty in completing all the arrangements. The *Great Eastern* ship was to form part of the work. We had not been able to do anything with her, and the company was wound up, the bondholders being in possession. She was put up to auction in Liverpool. Mr. Brassey, Mr. Barber, and myself, being the largest bondholders (the bonds in the whole amounting to £100,000), we then determined to buy her if she went for £80,000 or less, and Mr. Barber went down to Liverpool to attend the sale, when, strange to state, the ship was sold to us for £25,000. We offered the bondholders the option of coming in to form a new company, allowing them to come in, taking shares equal to the amount of their bonds as fully paid up. This the greater number did, and we paid the others their proportion of the £25,000 for which she sold. I then arranged with the Telegraph Construction Company (the company we had formed for laying the Atlantic cable) to charter the ship to them, taking payment in cable shares to the extent of £50,000 for the work, they to make all the alterations and pay all expenses. I was elected chairman of the Ship Company, Mr. T. Brassey, junr.,[2] and Mr. Barber being the other directors. Our Telegraph Construction Company was formed in April 1864, and we at once set to work in making preparations for the manufacture of the cable. I spent a great deal of time, and took much interest in it. We brought the ship from Liverpool to Sheerness in July to fit her for the work. I came round in her, and spent a few pleasant days at sea. The remainder of the year was very fully occupied in our preparations, and I often visited the ship at Sheerness. Putting the cable tanks in her made a great havoc in her internal arrangements.

On September the 22nd, 1864, my old and good friend Mr. Saunders died. He was one of the most able of our railway men, and in his time had probably had a greater amount of influence than any other. He was a perfect gentleman, and much liked by all the officers; we presented him with a very handsome testimonial in January. We had worked together for nearly my whole life, and never had a disagreement. He was always a good friend to his brother officers, and a man of high honour.

1865.—As Parliament was to be dissolved this year, I had to begin my canvas, having been invited to stand for Cricklade. I went to Swindon on the 3rd March to meet a few of the leading workmen, and appoint a committee. It was necessary I should make this canvas early, as the cable work was progressing fast, and I intended to go out with the ship, and might not even be in England at the time of the election, as happened to be the case.

I left the Great Western in September 1864, on which occasion the officers and servants of the company determined to present me with an address, and to make a present to my wife. The 3rd of June 1865 was the day fixed for my receiving it at Swindon. Great preparations had been made, and everything was done to show their kindly feelings towards me. I hope those who succeed me will value that address more than anything I can leave behind me, and also preserve the brooch and earrings as heirlooms in the family for ever. Man can receive no higher reward on earth than that of the goodwill and esteem of those with whom he has been associated through life, and my life had been passed in daily communication, both as master and brother officer, with those who gave expression to their feelings on this occasion. I count this 3rd of June as the brightest day in my life.

All things being ready for the cable expedition, I joined the ship at Sheerness on the 10th July. We expected to sail on the 12th, but did not actually sail until the 15th. The work of the ship was all ready in time, but the cable department were a little behind time. Captain James Anderson, of the Cunard service, had been appointed our captain, and future experience fully justified the choice. I found him a most able man. While I was on board the ship, the election at Cricklade took place. The nomination was on the 12th July; at this Lord Eliot and myself were elected by show of hands. The poll took place on the 13th, when Goddard polled 978, Gooch, 879, Eliot, 773.

July 7th.

I begin my journal of my American trip to-night, because I have now closed all my business matters, and must devote my time to the great work we have in hand. The work has the best wishes and prayers of all who know of it; its success will open a useful future for our noble ship, lift her out of the depression under which she has laboured from her birth, and satisfy me that I have done wisely in never losing confidence in her; and the world may still feel thankful to my old friend Brunel that he designed and carried out the construction of so noble a work. God grant all may work together for the happiness and welfare of mankind. I already begin to feel at home in my cabin, and that I am severed from old England. To-day I had a few lines of good wishes from some of my old and kind friends. It is pleasant to feel I am not forgotten. I will ever look forward to a happy return to all that is dear to me in England, with the hope that I may receive well-earned congratulations. It is a bright starlight night.

Wednesday, July 12th.

To-day is the nomination day at Cricklade. I have often wondered how matters have passed off, and wished we were in telegraphic communication with Swindon, and whether my absence will have any effect upon the result. Yet, if I knew it would have, I am certain I would have been here all the same. There is no comparison between the importance of the two works. My getting into Parliament or not will make no earthly difference to anybody, and to myself, the not doing so will add much to my comfort, and probably health; yet, having made the attempt, I will be disappointed if I fail.

Friday night, July 14th.

Well, I sleep to-night as an M.P. Do I feel any happier? No. Has it in any way satisfied an ambition? I say no, for I do not feel I ever had any particular ambition for the honour. I value it chiefly for the warm-hearted feelings it has called forth in those who have been associated with me for a long, long time, and it is a sequel to the kind reception given to me a little time ago; but I look back upon that reception as more honourable than this. Having, however, taken the office, I pray God it may enable me to do some good for my fellow-creatures, and I will endeavour to do my duty, and am grateful to those who have voted for me. What a change in one's life may be produced by a few hours! All the morning my mind has been very anxious, now it is at rest, and I have only one anxiety left, viz., the success of the cable, the most important of all.

Saturday night, July 15th.

This has been a lovely day, and put us all into good spirits at so fine a start. We weighed our anchor at 12.15, and have, so far, made a slow but pleasant voyage. A couple of stays in one of the screw-boilers gave way just before starting, and we had to take out the fires to get new ones put in. As we started and came along the coast large numbers of pleasure parties in all kinds of craft came off from the shore to have a look at us and give us a cheer. If the cheering and good wishes of the people could make this ship a success, she ought to be most perfect in that way. Go where she will, the voices of the people are raised in her praise. It has been a most enjoyable sail down the coast, the sunset was glorious, and now the sky is one blaze of light from the stars. We are now off Folkestone; the lights of the towns of Dover and Folkestone look very pretty from the sea. All seems to go well. We left our moorings drawing 28.6 feet forward and 34.6 feet aft, mean 31.6 feet. The paddle engines have not been making more than six and a quarter revolutions, and the screw twenty-eight, our speed through the water being only six knots. Before another cable is laid we must have extra boilers put into the ship, as we ought to have a larger margin of power. I also think there is still a good deal of foulness on her bottom.

Sunday, July 16th.

We have improved our speed a little to-day, having obtained seven knots, the paddles going six and a quarter and the screw about thirty.

I spent all the morning sitting on the paddle-box watching the gambols of that miserable *Caroline*,[3] as the seas break over her and wash along her decks; and one moment she is raised high in the air, and the next is almost lost to view down in the hollows of the waters. I pity those on board, and they must envy us, as we sit quietly looking at them with scarcely any motion in our noble ship.

Tuesday, July 18th, 12 P.M.

We have been on the bridge most anxiously watching the *Caroline:* it was fearful to see her. At one moment the light on her mast was lost below our stern, and the next it was shooting up high into the sky, at others, describing an arc of nearly one-third of a circle. I trust she will weather the night safely. There are about fifteen people on board of her, and our expedition rests upon the shore-end of the cable she has on board. If we lose this, we are done for several weeks. It was a great act of folly to put it into such a vessel. The night is cold, wet, and wild. I envy those who are now quietly in bed in dear old England: there is little rest for any one in this ship. We hope to reach Valencia by 6 in the morning, and I pray God the *Caroline* may also gain her port in safety. The speed of this ship is not affected by the wind, nor does the weight of the *Caroline* seem to have any effect upon us. We are now off Bantry Bay, making for the Skelling's light. I may as well lie down and rest my legs, at any rate. A star gleams out of the drifting clouds now and then.

BEAR HAVEN, BANTRY BAY, *Wednesday, July* 19*th.*
We arrived off Valencia this morning at 6 A.M. The night up to about 4 had continued very stormy. At that time the two ropes of the *Caroline* chafed through, and she was left to her own resources. Fortunately the weather moderated, and we had the great pleasure of seeing her get into harbour. The two war steamers, the *Sphinx* and *Terrible*, were also lying off near Valencia waiting for us. As it will take a couple of days at least (even if the weather is fine enough to do the work at all) to lay the shore-end, the captain has determined to run into this bay and wait. It is a long way from our work, being about eight hours' steaming. We therefore, as soon as the *Caroline* was safe, turned round and retraced our steps. The day turned out beautifully fine, and it was a delightful sail along the wild and beautiful coast of Kerry. The Skelling rocks are very fine, one being 740 feet high. There are also two beautiful rocks called the Bull and the Cow; they have fine

natural arches through them. We arrived at our anchorage here at five o'clock; it is a well-sheltered place, but it looks rather serious to see this big ship so closely surrounded by land. A mountain just opposite to her seems to be very high; its top is generally capped with clouds, and it rises very steep from the water. Brassey and several of our party, including the press, left us after dinner. They started in a large sailing boat to go 17 miles up the bay to Bantry. When they will get there is a very doubtful thing.

BANTRY BAY, *July* 20*th, Thursday.*
We are still lying here waiting for the laying of the shore-end. The two war-steamers have joined us, leaving Valencia this morning at 9 A.M., and say the weather was then calm.

ATLANTIC, *Sunday, July* 23*rd.*
I had just fallen asleep last night when a loud knock at my cabin door awoke me, and, after spending some seconds in trying to recollect where I was, and endeavouring to get out of bed on the side next the cabin partition, I got up and found a messenger had come from Valencia Bay to say they were laying the shore-end. The fires were at once lighted, and we left Bantry Bay at 2 A.M., reaching the *Caroline* at 10 A.M. Steps were immediately taken to make the splice, which was completed at 5.30, and we got fairly away on our voyage. A glorious day, nothing could have been finer, and our cable is now running out at the rate of nearly six knots per hour, the *Terrible* being on our port and the *Sphinx* on our starboard bows, about a half-mile from us. It was a beautiful and interesting scene all day as we lay together on the waters of the Atlantic, about twenty-five miles from the land, the two war-steamers, the *Caroline* and the *Great Eastern*. Mid-day, the *Hawk* came off to us with Canning,

Sir Robert Peel, the Knight of Kerry, and others, amongst them friend Barber. About four o'clock matters were so near ready that the ship was cleared of visitors, and, as we started, every one on board the ship thought it necessary to cheer until I think their lungs must have ached. It was an exciting scene. All our machinery works admirably, and I see no human reason why we should not in twelve days land it safely in Trinity Bay. Fine weather is predicted by all, and we are now satisfied it must be bad weather indeed which will seriously impede our work.

Monday, July 24th, noon.

What a change a few hours may make in our hopes, in our confidence. Last night I went to bed perfectly satisfied all was going as well as it was possible for anything to do, but at three this morning was awoke by one of the ship's guns, and on getting up to look out of my window, I found the paddle engines were not going. I then made up my mind something was wrong and went on deck. There I learned the cable had become defective. Some hours had been spent in trying to discover the place where the fault is. About this there is still some difference of opinion amongst the electricians. They vary from about ten miles back to the shore-end. The cable has been cut, and we are now getting it on board again, but very slowly, and if we do not succeed better in getting steam, it will be the work of several days. The early part of the day has been wet, but it has cleared up again. This has not served to raise our spirits. It is so far fortunate that this fault has shown itself in shallow water, so enabling us to pick up the cable again. After going on deck this morning, I went to lay down again for a couple of hours, and paid dearly for it by having a wretched dream that our expedition had all gone to the bad. I was so glad to wake up and find it but a dream.

Fortunately there is neither sea nor wind. We must keep up our hearts and yet hope for the best.

10 P.M.

The hauling-in of the cable has been going on very slowly, not quicker than about half-a-knot per hour, but our electricians seem more confident that the fault exists at the time the first intimation was given of, it, or about 10 or 12 miles back from the point where the cable was cut; we had gone about 78 miles from the land. If the 12 miles is the extent of what we have to take up, we may hope to accomplish this by three or four o'clock in the morning. I trust it may be so. We have telegraphed into Valencia for the *Hawk* to come to us, and for the *Caroline* to go out to the shore-end splice. It has been an anxious and a weary day. I shall be truly glad when we have discovered the cause of our difficulty. Our hauling-in engine is not equal to the work, and hence our very slow progress; it wants at least 50 per cent. more power. I can do no good on deck, and the night has come on wet with a small rain, but here we have been all day on the wide Atlantic, not an object visible beyond the two war-steamers lying near us. We certainly are not overlooked by the public, yet I can fancy if our difficulty is known in London it will have a very important effect on Atlantic-cable shares. This I do not care about; I still believe our work is to be done, and we will yet land the cable in good working order in the bay of Heart's Content. God grant it may be so, and then will our hearts be indeed content. I shall now see if I can get a few hours' sleep.

Tuesday, July 25th.

I do not know that I ever experienced the sensation of joy as I did this morning. Just as we finished breakfast at 8.30 a

message came down from the deck to tell us the cause of the
fault had come on board. Oh, what happy news it was, for
half-an-hour before, the captain, Canning, and I, had agreed
it was useless to waste more time in hauling in the cable; we
had only got in ten miles since yesterday morning when we
first began, and the electricians seemed so uncertain in their
calculation we thought it hopeless to persevere, and had
settled to cut the cable and go again to our starting-point.
Nay, I think we would have done so then, but Canning had
been connecting another boiler to our hauling-in engine
so as to give us more power, and the steam was not quite
ready to try its effect, which Canning wished to do in case
we might need it in deeper water. This slight circumstance
saved us. On examining the cable, the cause of the fault
was found: a piece of the steel-wire used in the cable had
been forced into it, and had made a hole in the core. The
question that naturally occurred to us was: had this been
done wilfully, or was it an accident? I examined the wire with
a magnifying-glass, and, as both ends were sharp and ragged,
it was clear it could not have been done by a hammer, nor
was it possible for a man to push it in with his fingers; there
were no marks of a pair of pliers having been used, so that
we came to the conclusion, and I think a correct one, that it
had fallen upon the coil of the cable, and the sharp end had
entered the outer tarry strands of the covering sufficiently
to carry it through the paying-out machinery, and that, in
passing through that, it had been forced in by the pressure
of the drums; the position of it also agreed with the part
of the cable that passed out at the time when the fault first
showed itself. It was a very satisfactory thing to feel this was
the case, as had it been a wilful injury we knew not whom to
suspect, and would have felt a constant dread of a repetition
of it. All hands were immediately set to work to get a fresh

splice made, and the cable carried out over the stern. This was complete at 2 P.M. The captain and I were standing together on the paddle-box as he was straining ahead to get the ship on her proper course, and just as this was finished we were coming down, I to my cabin to write the account of the morning's work, and had just expressed our thankfulness to Providence, when we saw Canning coming towards us calling out "Stop the ship." My heart seemed to sink within me, and he told us all signals through the cable had stopped; I felt as though I could have jumped into the sea. Oh, what a cast down it was! We then tried all the joints on board to see if any mistake had been made in making them, but no, all was right. We then cut off the two tanks to see if connection could be obtained through the one. This did not help us, and it was necessary to begin to make preparations to take the cable on board again. I felt so wretched that I went down to my cabin to lie down, for my head ached, and, if I could only fall asleep and forget for an hour, I thought it would be a relief. Sleep I found impossible. I tried to read. This was little better, but in about twenty minutes O'Neil came into my cabin and said the electricians had got some signal through the cable, and had hopes of doing better. I at once went on deck, and, after a most anxious half-hour's suspense, it was found all right, the cause being some neglect or mistake at Valencia in not carrying out the instructions. This is the excuse the electricians on board make. What a miserable two hours they have caused us! But thank God, all is now perfect, and we made a fresh start at 4 P.M., since when the cable has been going out at about six miles per hour in as satisfactory a manner as possible. The weather has fortunately been very fine. There is a heavy ocean swell running, but it does not affect us; the *Terrible* and the *Sphinx* dip their noses into it pretty deep. Our splice to-day was made in lat. 51° 58', long. 12° 9', or about seventy miles from the coast of Ireland. The cable is reported to-night in a most satisfactory state. I will endeavour not to hope too strongly, and so be better prepared for disappointment. It was very hard work the last thirty-six hours.

Wednesday, July 26th.

All has gone on exceedingly well to-day, the cable going out steadily at 6½ to 7 miles per hour, and we are now in deep water, or about 2000 fathoms. At noon to-day we were in lat. 52° 14', long. 15° 11', having put out 192 miles of cable. There has been a strong wind all day until four o'clock. It came from the south-west, with small rain, but has gradually got round to the north of west, and dry weather is prognosticated. The sea has been high, but very short, so that this ship has been like an island. The *Terrible* has been washing her decks over her bows all day. The *Sphinx* stopped this morning to take soundings, and she does not seem to be able to get up to us again, as she was just visible in the distance before dark. The cable tests have been very good. I like our captain very much. He is calm and clear in doing his work all through our troubles, though, like us all, he was very anxious, yet, unlike many captains, he had a cheerful and pleasant word for everybody. He also seems to have complete command over all his officers.

Thursday, July 27th.

All has prospered with us to-day, the day having been clear and bright, but a stiff breeze making the walk on the paddle-box bridges rather a windy job. At noon to-day we were in lat. 52° 34', long. 19° 1', having run since yesterday 142 miles, making a total distance from Valencia of 320 miles. There have been 351½ miles of cable laid, exclusive of an additional six miles caused by the loss of our course at the fault. It is now passing out at 7¼ miles per hour, with about 8½ per cent. of slack, making the speed of the ship about 6¾. The poor *Sphinx* has not gained upon us at all. She is still visible on the horizon. The *Terrible* keeps pace with us. The ship is now about in even keel. To-morrow night she will be up in the stern. There is a pretty heavy sea running.

Friday, July 28th.

Everything has gone on well with us to-day. At noon we were in lat. 52° 48' and long. 23° 16', having run 155.5 miles since yesterday, and payed out 174 miles of cable. All the machinery for this is working exceedingly well, and the cable is running out about seven miles per hour. The day has been bright and fine, with a strong head wind. All goes on so well, it is difficult to get through the day. The night is very fine, and the sun set beautifully. The moon has also just gone down, but the stars shine brightly. I wonder how they are in England; whether in that land of fogs (sometimes) it is clear there. Fogs or no fogs, I should like to be able to go through our cable and spend a day there. Patience, and I trust this will come in due course. Now for an hour's read in bed. Good night.

Saturday, July 29th.

This has been a most anxious afternoon, having had another fault in the cable. All had gone as well as could be until 20 past 1, when all signals with the shore ceased, showing a much more serious fault than the last. We were at the time laying the cable in 2000 fathoms water, at a depth of over two miles. It was a very doubtful question whether it would be possible to raise it again from that depth; the trial, however, was worth the making. Fortunately the sea is perfectly smooth, so that we had that important fact in our favour. At 9.30 to-night we succeeded in getting the fault on board, and have good signals at present from the shore; the only difficulty now is to get the splice made and the cable safely into the water again. This will require three or four hours, and it may be better to wait for daylight if the weather keeps as calm as it is. Our good captain is most anxious and attentive; he has never left the bridge since this trouble began, and will, I have no doubt, remain there until all is again in work. These are indeed very anxious hours, so much hangs upon this little thread we are laying at the bottom of the Atlantic—so much of credit and so much of value in the work, that my mind can, even when all is going well, never feel free from great anxiety. If it please God to make this work a success, I shall not again go out on a cable-laying expedition across the deep waters of the Atlantic. It is a defect, I think, in our machinery arrangements that we have not fixed our hauling-in gear in the stern of the ship— in fact, made the paying-out gear do the double duty if needed. With this ship I feel certain it might safely be done, and much time and risk consequent upon passing the end of the cable backwards and forwards along the whole length of the ship saved. I shall go to bed and get some sleep if I can until the new splices are made, and trust that to-morrow we will be going on all right again. It is a calm, foggy night, with a small rain; this has been the weather most of the day since about ten o'clock. At noon to-day we were in lat. 52° 38', long. 27° 40'. We have paid out 707 miles of cable, and have come from Valencia 634.4 miles, leaving us 1028.6 yet to do before reaching Newfoundland. A newspaper was published on board to-day edited by O'Neil; it caused some fun at lunch, but since our fault showed itself no one has been in any spirits for fun. I think I will not let fun enter

my thoughts for an hour until this work is either completed
or a failure. Good night.

Sunday, July 30th.

The splice was made this morning at three. It caught in the
drum, and was so much damaged it was necessary to cut it
out and make another. This was not complete until 8 A.M.,
when we steamed ahead all right, insulation capital, and
all has gone on well since. We only made 25 miles progress
during the twenty-four hours, so that our position at noon
to-day was very little changed. The morning was dreadfully
wet, and it has been very cold all day, but the rain ceased
about ten. We had church service this afternoon at 2.30,
and I feel certain many grateful hearts were there; for no
sooner had the fault shown itself yesterday than the wind
went down and the ocean became calm as a lake, and so it
continued until we were again under steam this morning,
when a fresh breeze sprang up, and has since continued. Had
we had this breeze during the night, there is no doubt we
would have lost our cable.

Monday, July 31st.

As yesterday was Sunday, we did not examine the piece of
cable in which the last fault occurred until to-day. A piece of
wire has been run quite through the cable, touching one of
the iron wires in the coating, and also the conductor. But for
these two faults, we would have by to-day been nearly across,
and our anxiety at an end. We have had no difficulty of any
other kind. The precaution we have taken is to remove from
the tanks all strange men, and do the best we can with the
few trustworthy men we have. I fear, on this trip, no more
can be done; but it is a warning for the future, which I trust
our engineers will not lose sight of. We are now just about

half way across, having paid out at twelve to-day 930 miles. We are in lat. 52° 9', long. 31° 53'. The weather has been calm, and the ocean as smooth as a mill-pond.

We saw a ship near us this evening. It created quite a sensation, as we have not had anything to look at over the mighty expanse of water.

Tuesday, August 1st.

All has gone on well to-day with the cable. We have paid out 1081 miles, and are 946 miles from Valencia, so that we have considerably passed the half-way house, being now, or rather at mid-day, only 717 miles from our destination. At noon the lat. was 51° 52' 30", long. 36° 3' 30". The weather has been very fine. Sea quite smooth. To-night the wind has got up a little, but nothing to produce the least motion in the ship. I have to go on watch to-night in that wretched tank at twelve o'clock. It is anything but an agreeable job to stand for two hours in a tank of cable covered with tar, and, like a girl with a skipping-rope, jump over the cable as it runs out, say every minute, or else sit on the edge of an iron bar with your legs upraised above the cable. The night is cloudy and dark. The deck of our ship has a very irregular look, lighted up with long lines of lamps, more like the streets of a town than a ship.

Wednesday, August 2nd.

All is over, I fear, for this year, and our cable is gone. At 5.30 this morning a fault was discovered and the ship stopped. Steps were at once taken to haul the cable in again. The depth was very great, being over 2000 fathoms. Two miles were got in very well, at 1.30 the cable broke a few yards from the ship, and all our labour and anxiety is lost. We are now dragging to see if we can by chance recover it, but of this I have no hope, nor have I heart to wish. I shall be glad if I can sleep and for a few hours forget I live. This is indeed a sad and bitter disappointment. A couple of more days and we would have been safe. God's will be done.

Thursday, August 3rd. 11 A.M.

I went to bed at nine last night, taking a book with me to read, but it was idle; my eyes might be on the page, but my thoughts were at the bottom of the Atlantic; and I put out my candle, and at once fell into a sound and comfortable sleep which lasted until daylight this morning. Oh, what a hard and bitter disappointment this is to us all, more hard because so slight a matter has caused it. We have not seen the third fault, and we do not know therefore if it was like either of the former ones. The effect was like that of the first; it was a puncture into the copper wire, but there was no actual metallic connection between the copper and the iron wires. At the time of the fault, Mr. Field was in the tank, it being his watch, and one of the men heard a click as if a piece of projecting wire struck the ring of the crinoline, and he called out "broken wire" to the man on deck. He did not hear it, and the word was not passed on to the men at the paying-out machinery to relieve the pulleys. Immediately notice was given from the electrician's room that the insulation was bad, and the ship was stopped. At the same time that this occurred, one of the men in the tank picked up off the coil a short piece of the wire of the cable, about one and three-quarter inches long, with one end freshly broken and the rest rusted down considerably in size, forming a taper piece of wire, quite sufficient to have punctured the core of the cable, and been thrown out in passing from the tank; and as the effect on the cable was such as this would produce, it is reasonable to conclude that it was the cause. If so, then we have three accidents, all very simple in themselves, all very probable, and all very simply prevented in the future. I did not know before that the fracture of these steel wires was a very common occurrence in the manufacture and coiling of the cable in the ship, but there is no difficulty in coming to the conclusion that these solid steel wires are the mistake and defect in the cable, and had they been a strand of very fine material, a fracture could not have formed a puncturing instrument. When they break they often assume this position.

And it has been the practice to secure the end down by a piece of sewing; but as the fracture is more likely to take place as the cable is running out, no one sees it, and the result must in some cases, out of the many that occur, be to drive them into the cable at the paying-out machinery. We have now about 1100 miles of cable on board; I would cover this entirely with a sewing of hard cord, and make any new cable, as I said, with strand, instead of solid wire. Nor have I any doubt that such a cable would be laid without any difficulty; we would have had none but for this one defect. Weather having very little influence on this ship, and however bad it may be, I have no doubt the only effect would be to drive us a little out of our course, and so consume some more cable, there is nothing that can throw doubt on the possibility of laying a cable across the Atlantic; and as the insulation of this cable has gradually improved as it was put into deep water, until it is now twelve times better than the contract standard, a cheaper material might be used in the outer coatings of the core, and the whole cable be laid at a much less cost. These will be all matters to think over and discuss when we get back. After the fault was discovered yesterday, we at once got the cable round to the hauling-in machine at the bows of the ship, and a little over two miles was got in with great ease, the cable showing much less strain upon it than we found the first time. It was then cut on board to see if the fault had come in. This not being the case, we began to haul in again, but by that time, one o'clock, the wind had changed and freshened a little, and it was more difficult to keep the ship's head in the position wanted. The cable caught on one of the projecting hawse holes and across the stem. To relieve this, a man was sent down to make a chain fast to the cable below it. This was done and the cable freed, and the part where the chain was fastened had been pulled inwards three or four yards, when the cable broke. I have no doubt the chain had damaged it; it was a dangerous thing to use, but I am told a rope would not hold. The ship was taken back about ten miles and a few miles to windward of our course, and grapnel irons lowered with 2500 fathoms of line, and the ship allowed to drift across the course we believed the cable to lie. At daylight this morning we had drifted sufficiently far to have crossed the cable, and we commenced to haul up our line. One of the wheels in the machine broke and delayed us some time, as it was necessary to make use of the anchor capstan. We are now slowly getting it up, and from the strain there is good reason to hope we have hold of the cable. I cannot say I have the least hope of success, but we would not have been satisfied to leave it without a trial; but I fear, even if we have hold of it, the strain will be too much, and the line will fail before we get it on board. It is very extraordinary how the weather seems to favour us; in all our difficulties the winds and sea have become calm. When I went to bed yesterday morning at 2.30, it was blowing very hard, and the sea running high—in fact, as dirty a night at sea as you would care to be out in; yet by six o'clock it was perfectly calm, and has remained nearly so until now, and beautifully fine. The last couple of hours have not been so fine; there is both more wind and sea, and the glass has gone down. It also rains, and looks dirty. A few hours will tell us whether we get the cable on board or not, although we will probably make one more attempt if this fails. There will be many anxious minds in England to-day, as I daresay this morning's papers would state the cable was gone or in serious difficulties. How one short hour has buried all our hopes, the toil and anxiety of the two last years all lost! This one thing, upon which I had set my heart more than any other work I was ever engaged in, is dead, and all has to begin again, because it must be done, and, availing ourselves of the experience of this, we will succeed. I must now return to England to receive the sympathy of my friends, not their congratulations, as I had so fondly hoped. The cable broke in lat. 51° 25', long. 39° 1'.

Thursday night, August 3rd.

There is no doubt we had hold of the cable this morning, and raised it 700 fathoms, when the strain was too much for our line, and it broke at one of the shackles. This occurred about twelve o'clock. We have resolved to try again, and have taken up a position nearer the end of the cable. Where we tried before was about twenty-five miles from the end. We are now about seven or eight miles, but unfortunately the wind has gone to the west, and as this would drift us in the exact line of the cable, it is no use letting down the grapnel iron, so here we are waiting for a change in the wind. It would not be safe to steam across it, as our speed would be too much. The day has been foggy, wet, and dreary, and the night is no better. I have just had a solitary ramble for half-an-hour on deck, and shall get to bed. Every one on board, since our accident, has been very low in spirits, none more so than O'Neil. I have not heard a note of music from him since, nor do any of them seem inclined for a rubber at whist, but they sit talking over our troubles. If we had each lost a dear friend, we could not be a more melancholy party. I certainly have no hope of getting up the cable. Two and a half miles is a great depth to fish. It takes us about two hours to get the line down, and double that time to lift it.

Friday night, August 4th.

This is the night we had fully calculated upon reaching sight of land, yet here we are still near the end of the broken cable. It was not until twelve o'clock to-day that observations could be taken to determine our exact position, since which time we have steamed up to this point, supposed to be exactly over the cable, and about seven miles from the broken end, and we have put down a buoy to mark the spot, and the ship is now steaming a few miles to windward to drop our grapnel iron, and so drift across the line of the cable, and see what we can do towards picking it up. I have no hopes, and feel we have now only one thing to do—to consider what is best to be done next year in the laying of another cable. It must be done, and I will not rest content until it is done. There is no difficulty in it, and further consideration and examination convinces me that our failure has arisen entirely from the solid wire in the present cable. It is very vexing to be told to-day by the electricians that the last fault was of such a trifling character that the cable would probably have worked well for many years had we left it in the water and gone on. It makes one very angry to think, to secure perfection we have lost the whole cable; yet I feel if the matter had been fully discussed whether we should leave the cable imperfect or try and repair the fault, as we had done twice before with success, we would have voted on the side of perfection. My own mind is quite convinced the injury was not caused by any person on board, but was the work of the cable itself. The day has been wet and dry alternately, but a very long one. We are not in spirits to get up any fun, and we go on all day discussing our misfortune, until I feel more weary than I would do after a hard day's work. This afternoon I heard the piano again, and to-night whist is being played, so that a portion of our party are getting reconciled to our fate, which is certainly a very hard one.

Monday night, August 7th.

We have had a very anxious day. When I went on deck this morning, the fog had all cleared away and the wind got round to the north, just in the direction we wished it. Steam was immediately got up, and we went away to the windward of the cable, and to a point determined by the captain and Moriarty[4] as one from which we would drift across the cable a couple of miles from the end. At twelve o'clock we began to lower the grapnel iron, and let out 2600 fathoms and allowed the ship to drift. We went on all the afternoon until about seven o'clock, when the increased strain on the dynamometer, which rose from 42 cwt. to 63 and 65, led us to hope we had hooked the cable. The ship also began to swing to it, we therefore began to haul up at about 7 P.M. After a very short time one of the wheels of the hauling-in machine broke, making it useless; we were therefore obliged to use the capstan, which is a very slow process, and will require fourteen or fifteen hours to get it in. I greatly fear our tackle is not equal to the work to be done, and do not allow my hopes to assume so sanguine a colour.

Tuesday, August 8th.

What I fully expected has happened again. After hauling at our cable all night and getting it 1000 fathoms from the ground, at 7.30 this morning another of the shackles of the grapnel line broke. The morning was very fine until middle of the day. We put down another buoy to mark the spot we had been lifting, and after a long consultation with the captain and Canning, we determined to make one more try with the best of the materials we have on board, do away with all the wretched shackles, and get all the additional security we can muster; this will require a couple of days. If we then fail, we must at once return direct to Sheerness. The time of making the trial is very uncertain, as we need not only calm weather, but that the little wind we want should be either from the north or the south, or nearly so, to drift us over the cable at right angles. The weather this afternoon has completely changed. It first began to rain about two o'clock, and the wind gradually got up until noon. It is now blowing half a gale, and the sea is rising very fast.

Wednesday, August 9th.

The gale last night was a very sharp though short one, and the ship was steamed 36 miles into it. Her head was turned round at six this morning, when the wind had very much diminished, but the sea was very high. The rain cleared off and we have had a fair day, with an occasional look at the sun fortunately, or I do not know how we would have found the buoy we put down yesterday morning. This, however, was very cleverly managed by the captain and Moriarty, and at five o'clock we were close beside it. The science of navigation is a very wonderful one. To me the ocean looks only a pathless sea, yet these navigators will bring you to the same spot from any distance and from any quarter, as though there was a huge signal-mast to direct them. The rolling was pretty lively to-day, as much as five degrees each way.

Thursday, August 10*th.*

We got our position this morning about seven to drop our grapnel iron, and it was let down by 9 A.M. 2500 fathoms. There was a very moderate north wind blowing, but a current of about a mile per hour against us, so that it was necessary to set all our sail to get sufficient drift upon the ship. She looks very grand with the sail set. In spite of it all we drifted very slowly, and without, I fear, getting hold of the cable. We ought to have got it between one and two o'clock, but the dynamometer showed us no sign of any great increase in the strain, and at five it was settled to pull up the grapnel and try again to-morrow. It is now coming up slowly and steadily with a strain of about 60 cwt. Some hope we have the cable, but I fear not. Another five hours will get the grapnel up. It is anxious and weary work, and, following day after day, is very depressing.

Friday, August 11*th.*

Our last hope has gone, if it existed, and our ship's head is now turned towards home under full steam. When the line came in early this morning, it was found that the chain attached to the grapnel had fouled it, and had been dragging it along the ground the wrong way, so that there was no chance of our hooking the cable. The grapnel and almost 400 fathoms of the line had been dragging along the bottom, and came up covered with chalky-looking ooze, and showing that the soundings giving 2000 fathoms are correct. Immediate steps were taken to make another haul across the line of cable, and at four o'clock the strain on the dynamometer showed we had hooked it, when we immediately began to haul it in. This went on very steadily and satisfactorily until about 7.30, by which time 700 fathoms of line had come in, and the cable was about 300 fathoms from the bottom. We were all standing near the capstan, speculating on the chance of a successful result and our yet reaching Trinity Bay, when a loud report like that of a gun, and the whiz of the end of the rope, told us precisely what had happened and brought our hopes and trials to a conclusion. It was a hard case, and cast a sad gloom over us for a time; but there was the fact, and the conviction that even if we had enough rope left for another trial (nearly six miles having now been lost) it was useless. A signal was at once made to the *Terrible* to send a boat to us, and informing them of the result. Lieutenant Prowse was soon on board, and we prepared as quickly as we could a short account of our misfortunes for the *Terrible* to take to Newfoundland, and telegraph on to the American press. Russell had also kept a copy of his daily journal written up, which was also sent, so that in a few days the full account of our voyage will be known in America, and people's minds set at rest. The weather, as was the case in every instance when it was important to us, had been all we could desire all day, and the sea quite calm, but no sooner had the line broken, than the wind began to blow hard from the south with heavy rain, and in an hour the sea became covered with foam, and a state of weather existed that would have rendered our hauling in the cable quite impossible. I fear the season will be too late for us to be ready to pick up and complete the present cable this year, and it will have to be postponed until the spring. I wonder whether I will come or not; my present feeling is not to do so, yet I have a strong longing to witness the completion of the work I have begun. Well, we will see. I will make no present resolutions; as an M.P. I may not find it possible. I expect this honour will be a great bother to me and a great tie. Well, I had made up my mind to do it, and do not now care how soon it is at an end.

Tuesday, August 15th.

How time softens all disappointment! I begin to look back upon our broken cable as a matter to be regretted, but not one to discourage me in the ultimate success of our work. It is true we have failed to complete the cable to Heart's Content; it is true we have laid 1200 miles of the most perfect cable ever laid under water; it is, I believe, true that we can come out with proper tackle and pick up the end, and go on to lay the next with certainty—this for a cost not exceeding £30,000. It is, therefore, no failure, but a postponement of our final triumph; we are not beaten, but checked, and the final result is as certain to my mind as it ever was. No doubt we were cast down by the fracture; it was very unexpected; but seeing, as we did from the first, the possibility of restoring it, why should we have made ourselves so miserable? The human mind, thank God, is very elastic, and soon recovers from any shock. We now feel to have only one thought, viz., the best way of completing our work, nothing doubting its success. We have had a large amount of excitement to-day, actually saw *two* ships; one passed close under our bows, the other at some distance. Our men having nothing to do, have been employed in getting the ship clean and all in ship-shape order and we certainly look all the better for it; in fact, we begin to look very smart, and will be like a new ship when we arrive at Sheerness. I hope we will have a good stiff westerly breeze to go up Channel, that we may show all the inhabitants of the towns on each side that we can still cut a dash with all our sails set, and show our noble old ship off to advantage. No stars, but a loving good-night.

CLEWER, *Sunday, August 20th.*

We left Brighton by the 11 A.M. train, and I reached Paddington at one. How nice the trees and green fields looked as we passed along. I left by the 2 P.M. train for Windsor, and found my wife had not returned from Cornwall, where she had been ten days with her sister. I had said I would not be home until Sunday, so that she did not return until last night. How nice Clewer is looking! How much I have enjoyed the quiet and beauty of this place to-day; both yesterday and to-day have been very fine.

Now what has been the real result of our voyage? These pages will show the many hopes and fears that filled my mind from day to day, and it will probably take many days of quiet thought to see all clear and what is best for the future. Our voyage has certainly not been lost to science. We have gained an amount of knowledge that could only be gained by such a failure as we have had. The money is not, I think, ill spent. We have proved to demonstration—

1. That a submarine cable can be laid between Ireland and Newfoundland.

2. That perfect and speedy messages at the rate of five to seven words per minute can be transmitted through the cable so laid.

3. That the insulation of a cable increases very much after its submersion in the cold water of the deep Atlantic, and that its conducting power is considerably improved thereby.

4. That the steam-ship *Great Eastern*, from her size and consequent steadiness, and from the control exercised over her by the joint use of the screw and paddles, renders it safe and practicable to lay a cable in any weather.

5. That the egress of a cable, in the course of being laid from the *Great Eastern*, may be safely stopped on the appearance of a fault, and with the paying out machinery being strengthened and made to recover, and so be used as hauling-in machinery, the fault may at once be lifted from the greatest depths of the Atlantic between Ireland and

Newfoundland, and cut out on board the ship, and the cable re-spliced and laid in perfect condition.

6. That with perfect hauling-in machinery and tackle a cable may be grappled for in any of these depths and hauled on board the ship with certainty.

7. That with the improved telegraphic instruments for long submarine lines, a speed of even eight words per minute may be obtained through such a circuit as the Atlantic cable of 1865. As the amount of slack actually paid out did not exceed 14 per cent., and as this included the additional amount caused by the faults, it will be even less, making the distance between Valencia and Newfoundland under 1900 miles.

8. That this cable, although capable of bearing a strain of eight tons, was not subjected to more than 14 cwt. in paying out into the deepest water of the Atlantic in which it is laid.

9. That there is no difficulty in mooring buoys in the deep water of the Atlantic, and that two so moored, even by a piece of the cable itself, rode out a gale.

10. That more than four miles of the cable have been recovered from a depth exceeding two miles, and that the insulation of the gutta-percha covered wire was in no way whatever impaired, either by the depth of water or the strain of about 80 cwt. to which it was subjected in hauling in, nor was the outer surface injured.

11. That the improved construction of this cable over that laid in 1858 shows an increase in the rate of signalling of at least 33 per cent.

12. That the electrical testing can be conducted at sea with such certainty as to discover the existence of faults in less than a minute of their production.

These are facts proved by our recent experience, and which may be said to have made certain that which was not only doubted before, but by many considered impossible.

On my return to London I was surprised at a proposal made to me to take the chair of the Great Western Railway. I was elected as chairman on the 2nd November 1865, and took the chair at the board on the 16th November.

1. It should be recorded here that in June 1861 the ship took out 2500 troops to Quebec.
2. Now Lord Brassey.
3. The *Caroline*, containing the shore end of the cable, was being towed by the *Great Eastern*.
4. Captain Moriarty, RN., assisted in the navigation in the expeditions of 1865 and 1866, and was created a C.B. for his services.

IV

THE ATLANTIC CABLE-LAYING EXPEDITION OF 1866

1866.—The cable scheme occupied very much of my thoughts in the commencement of the year. All means of raising the capital by the Atlantic Company had failed, and I saw no hopes of doing anything through their powers. Mr. Cyrus Field came over from America to work at it, and came to my house late one Sunday night in despair. I then proposed to him that we should start a new company, under an agreement with the Atlantic to find the capital and lay the cables, paying them any profits we might get beyond a fixed amount. This scheme was at once acted upon, and the Anglo-American Company was formed in March 1866; but the difficulty was still to raise the £600,000 required. I proposed to our board at the Construction Company, that each director should put his name down for £10,000 on a sheet of paper at once, to show the public that we had confidence in our scheme. This made some long faces, but I began the list with my name, and nine others added theirs, so that we had £100,000 round the table. This good start had the required effect, and we succeeded in raising the capital, the Construction Company taking a good deal of it, and set to work in earnest to fit out the *Great Eastern* and complete the new cable. Great consideration and attention was given to the machinery for hauling in the cable. Nothing could work better than our paying-out machinery had done; but we required entirely new machinery for hauling in, with good and powerful engines to work them. We also put one of these machines to work in connection with the paying-out gear, so that, in case of a fault showing itself, the cable could be at once hauled back, without cutting or disturbing it, from the paying-out machinery. Every other precaution we could think of from our former experience was taken; special dresses were prepared for the men to be employed in the tanks, so that they could not conceal any instrument by which damage might be done to the cable, although I do not believe the former faults were caused by wilful damage. A full consideration of the matter last year convinced me of this, and that the damage was caused by broken wires in the cable itself, sticking out and piercing it as it uncoiled from the tank. I had at one time made up my mind not to go out with the expedition this year, feeling unwilling to leave my duties at the Great Western; but as the time drew near, I determined to go, and I was afterwards very glad I did.

I took the chair at the Great Western shareholders' meeting on the 2nd March for the first time, and was glad to receive from the proprietors a kind and hearty reception. It gave me confidence, and I had no difficulty in stating on what principles I would manage the concern, viz., to avoid all further obligations with new lines and extensions, to make as far as possible friendly relations with adjoining companies, and to cut down all capital expenditure to a minimum. By the middle of June all matters connected with our cable expedition had been nearly completed, and I joined the ship at Sheerness on the 29th.

"GREAT EASTERN," *Friday, June 29th.*
Yes, I am again seated in this familiar cabin. What is my present hope? Is it the same as last year? Do I feel the same confidence? No. The hope is as strong, but not the confidence; the experience of last year showed me by what a slender thread our success hung, how little might destroy all our hopes. Yet are we this year provided with means we had not last time, and for want of which I think our enterprise failed; yet it was a great and uncertain work, and we must hope for the blessing of God upon our endeavours. This large party makes beds scarce. The day has been very hot, and the night is a glorious one, the moon shining so brightly over the water. I trust it is the sign of a fine voyage.

THE NORE, *Saturday, June 30th.*
This has been until evening a very hot day. We left our moorings punctually at the time fixed, viz., twelve o'clock, and the old ship was once more in motion. She moved out of the harbour beautifully, amid the cheers of all who could see her in the ships and on the shore, the guardship's band playing the parting tune of "Good-bye, sweetheart, good-bye."

Sunday, July 1st.
We passed Dover at 8.30 this evening, and there discharged our pilot into a small tugboat that had come out with some sightseeing people to have a look at us. Several of those on board of her did not seem particularly to enjoy it; it was very rough, and continues so; the wind sings through our rigging,

and it is too rough to be on deck except under shelter. We had church in the grand saloon; Moriarty read the service. Good night.

Monday, July 2nd.

The weather during last night was very rough, and the wind right ahead; we have consequently not made as good progress as we expected. We were off Brighton at eight in the morning, the St. Catherine's Head at two, and Portland Bill at nine. It has been blowing very hard all day, and we have had the satisfaction of seeing that we passed all the other steamers going in our direction, with the exception of the large American steamer the *Baltic;* she came out of Southampton, and gradually got past us a few minutes ago. We had a very narrow escape of a collision, just before I left the deck, with a very large ship; she seemed determined to sail right into us, and nearly succeeded; our ship's course was altered ten degrees to get out of her way. I am a little disappointed with the speed of the ship. Although we fancied her bottom was nearly clean, and that a couple of knots per hour extra speed would be obtained, we do not seem to have got it. Our distance run, up to twelve to-day, was only 145 miles. Last year we ran in the same time 147. I fancy the weather then quite calm, while we have had this year a half gale to contend against. She has burnt only 183 tons of coals this trip, as against 261 last year. I begin now to get a little accustomed to the noises in the ship. The first couple of nights it is not very easy to sleep; a great change from pretty Clewer in that respect. As they seem to be winding up in the saloon, I will also go to bed, and read for half an hour before I go to sleep. Good night.

Wednesday, July 4th.

We have not made much speed the last twenty-four hours. At noon we were in lat. 50° 55', long. 8°, the distance come since noon yesterday being 151 miles, the coals burnt, 203 tons. We are now off the Fastnet light, and have slowed the speed so as to spend our time till daylight for going into Bantry Bay. This has been a very rough day, blowing a heavy gale of wind against us, the sea running mountains high. For the first time, to my knowledge, the sea has come upon her decks. I was on the grating at the bow, looking over to see her bottom as the sea left her, when a huge sea struck her on the bow, and, mounting up her side, broke over us, giving me a good wetting. Very many seas struck her sponsons, and rushed up on to her paddle-box on the weather side. During the night I was often startled from my sleep by these seas. It sounded as though the paddle-wheel was broken and was smashing up its paddle-box. In spite of all this, the ship was comparatively steady, the ladies and others sitting about as though it was quite smooth. She rolled through an angle of about 5°, and pitched about 1½°. It was very beautiful to see such a mass as this ship rising and falling with the waves, like a yacht, only slow and graceful in her movements.

BANTRY BAY, *Friday morning, July 6th.*

We anchored here yesterday morning about seven o'clock, and are now hard at work coaling. We have 160 Irishmen assisting our own crew.

Several of our party left us to-day. I was very much pleased to see the name of the steam-tug we have in attendance on us. She came from Cork, and is called the *Brunel*. It is rather a curious coincidence that his name should turn up here in the midst of labours in which he has performed an important part. I hope it is an omen of success. Our party will be further reduced to-day. We will probably by Sunday settle down into our correct numbers. I am going up the Bay.

Sunday, July 8th.

When I sit and think over the work we have on hand, and all the many difficulties and uncertainties we have to contend with, my heart sometimes sinks, and a cloud of doubt will hang over me. God knows how we have striven for success, and it will be very hard if we fail. I cannot feel the same confidence I had last voyage; yet my reason and judgment tell me how much better we are prepared for our task; but the experience of our last voyage has shown me how easy it is to fail, how many things may occur that have not presented themselves to our minds, and arranged to provide against. I will try and hope that God will bless our undertaking. As I look at the young fellows on board, so full of life and fun, so free from care, I cannot help envying them their light hearts. A messenger has just come from Killarney with a message saying the shore was laid last night, so that we may get away as soon as our coaling is done.

Monday, July 9th.

The day opened with a little better prospect of fine weather, and by mid-day the fogs had in a great degree cleared away, with the exception of long banks of them hanging on the sides of the mountains. Captain Commerell[1] of the *Terrible* came on board, and we spent some time in discussing with him the programme of our proceedings. He enters heart and soul into the work. In our discussions it was very wonderful to hear these navigators speak of getting Greenwich time every day. In the *Great Eastern* we will get it direct from Greenwich as long as we are connected to the cable, and the actual loss or difference between Greenwich and Newfoundland will be only the one-twentieth part of a second. It is marvellous to think of.

THE ATLANTIC, *Friday, July* 13*th*.

We are once more fairly at work paying out the cable. We reached the buoy at the shore-end soon after daylight this morning, and found the other three ships waiting for us. There was a good deal of sea on, with a strong southerly wind, and it took some time to get into a position to pick up the buoy. This was done soon after eleven o'clock, and the end of the shore-end was brought on board at about twelve. The splice was made, also a piece of the shore-end cut out in which there was a kink, in about two and a half hours, so that about three o'clock the head of the ship was turned to the west, and we began to pay out the cable. All seems to work remarkably well. To stand and look at it, it is impossible to believe any difficulty exists. The aft hauling-in machinery also worked very well. There is ample power, and it is well under control. We are progressing at five knots per hour. The *Terrible* is a little ahead of us on the port side, the *Medway* a little astern, also on the port side, and the *Albany* is a little astern of us on the starboard side, so that we form quite a procession crossing the Atlantic. Nothing could have been more unfortunate for us than the weather. It rained up to the time of our starting very hard; for a few hours it cleared up, but is now a dirty wet night, inclined to be very thick. It has been some amusement to see the young fellows who have to go into the tanks in their fancy dress; they certainly look like convicts. We have arranged that every one who goes into the tanks has to put on this dress. It covers their whole person and fastens up the back, and is without pockets, so that no one can take anything into the tanks without its being seen. The *Racoon* lay along side of us until we started with the cable, and then steamed into Valencia with the reporters and some of our friends. I earnestly hope God will bless our great undertaking and permit us to carry it to a successful end. The next twelve or fourteen days will be most anxious ones to us all, and few of us will get much sleep. I cannot see why we should fail. I have tried often to find out a weak point, but in vain. My friends in England will now see our daily progress, and I have no doubt will look for the information with great anxiety.

Saturday, July 14th.

I have now been a full fortnight on board of the ship. It looks a long time since I left dear old England and all it contains so dear to me. The night has been a very variable one as to weather, a very thick fog during the early part of it, and we had the amusement of hearing our steam-whistle constantly blowing up to twelve o'clock; after which it cleared up, and this morning the weather was fine and bright, with a nice S.W. wind, all we could wish for cable-laying. The *Terrible* and the *Medway* were under sail. The *Albany* does not seem to value his coals, as he has not put up any sails. We had a message through from the shore during the night wishing us success. I suppose they must have been drinking our healths or their own pretty late, as it was after twelve o'clock when we got the message. The answer was sent this morning. We also had Greenwich time given to us at 11 after 10 this morning, and have given it to the other ships. Our position at noon was lat. 52° 0', long. 14° 0'. We have made 108.1 miles since making the splice yesterday, and paid out 115.08 miles of cable. The splice was made in about lat. 51° 50', long. 11° 6', or a distance from Valencia of 27.5 miles, the cable laid being 29.5 miles; so that we at nine to-day had run from Valencia 135.5 miles and payed out 144.58 miles of cable, equal 6.46 per cent. of slack, and our distance from Heart's Content is 1533.8 miles. We left Bearhaven with 7807 tons of coals. I hear a steamer passed us exceedingly close last night in the fog. She must have been astonished to see so many lights. It was fortunate she got through amongst us without any accident. We have had a very fine day, with a nice S.W. breeze, and the cable has gone out beautifully. We are now in deep water and all looks very well. The new moon to-night was visible and looked like fine weather. The stars are also very bright; the evening star shines into my cabin window. We are a very quiet party on board this year. We now have no music, nor do I see any one play at cards. We, I fancy, all feel anxious about our work. To-night we begin to use some of the old cable, about 260 miles of it, so that for the next two days I shall feel very anxious. I wish we had none of it on board. I know it to be full of broken wires, but hope at the slow speed we are going no accident will happen. There has been no accident on board to-day to give us any excitement, and our principal occupation is to stand and watch the cable entering the water so quietly and silently, I trust never to be seen again.

Sunday, July 15th.

We began to pay out the old cable this morning at 8.20; one broken wire showed itself, but otherwise it has gone on quite well so far. We have slowed the speed of the ship to a little under five knots per hour. The position of the ship to-day, lat. 52° 1' 15", long. 17° 29', distance run since yesterday 128 miles, and cable payed out 138.97 miles. We are 263 from Valencia, and 1406 from Heart's Content, so that we are gradually getting on. If all goes well until next Sunday, we will feel our work safe, as we will then be in shallow water.

Monday, July 16*th.*

Another glorious day has passed over our heads, and all
has gone well with the cable; by early to morrow morning
we will have payed out all the cable of last year, and I
shall feel much more comfortable to get to work upon
the new cable. The sea to-day has been one sheet of glass,
reflecting the ships accompanying us in its bright mirror,
not a ripple on its surface, while light clouds have shaded
us to some extent from the hot rays of the sun. To-night
I think the sunset was as beautiful a scene as mortal eyes
could look upon; all along the western horizon there was
a streak of yellow light below some dark clouds, and,
lighted up by the sun behind them, the effect was that of
a bright, beautiful country, and it was hard to believe it
was not land.

Tuesday, July 17*th.*

I am very glad to say we finished paying out the old cable
this morning at 7 a.m. It removes a great deal of anxiety
from my mind, as we were having an average of three broken
wires every watch. The speed at which we payed it out no
doubt saved us some trouble, as it was possible for the men
in the tank to examine each coil before it went out, and in
some cases to get a lapping round the broken wire. The slow
speed caused us to lay more slack than we wished, but this
is a small evil compared with a fault. We had a great fright
this afternoon; the danger bell in the tank rang, and notice
was given immediately on deck and to the engine-rooms
to reverse the engines and stop the ship. This was all done
very quickly, and in a little over her own length, when it was
found the cause was a careless act on the part of one of the
clerks in the electricians' room, who, without knowing it,
had put his arm on the key which gave the signal. All were

thankful there was no real cause for danger, and the ship went on again.

Wednesday, July 18th, 3 P.M.

When I finished my journal last night at about ten o'clock, I certainly began to feel more confidence in our success than I had done before, the new cable appeared to be going out so well, and it hardly seemed possible for anything to occur to endanger our enterprise. I went to bed more satisfied than I had done before. But what poor weak mortals we are! As I lay reading only a short time after getting into bed, I fancied I heard a change in the noise of the ship. I listened, and hoped it arose from a lull in the wind, and tried to read on, but knew not what I was reading; I felt that sinking of the heart as though it would stop beating, and in a moment or two I was obliged to get up and look out of my port, but the beating of the heavy sea against the side of the ship and the roaring of the wind prevented my being able to tell whether the paddles were at work or not; so I at once put on my clothes and went on deck. It was pitch dark and raining very hard, and blowing very roughly. I looked down the paddle-engine-room and found them standing; I then went aft, and found a large quantity of the cable on the deck all entangled like a piece of thread, and the ship stopped, holding on by the cable with stoppers. It appears that as the cable was running out of the coil it had caught two of the lower coils, and pulled it up with it in two long bights. All hands were hard at work trying to get it unravelled, while the captain was doing his best to ease the strain on the cable at the stern, of the ship—a very difficult task, as the wind blew so hard. It certainly was an awful night, and such a task seemed hopeless. It took nearly two hours to get the ravelled part of the cable back into the tank. When it was eased gradually over the stern, the delay before getting into our course again was about three hours, and a most anxious time it was. All seemed lost, and, from the state of the weather, had we put a buoy to mark the spot, it might have drifted a considerable distance, and we of course had no chance of getting any observation. The same fouling took place at six o'clock this morning, but the men in the tank were able to free it before it was lifted out of the tank, and the ship was only stopped a few minutes. Every precaution we can think of has been taken to prevent it for the future; but it is clear that this new cable free from the tar has a tendency to spring up from the lower coil. We have further reduced the speed of the ship, and if we have any more of it, must have it all served out of the tank by hand. A few days' delay is of no consequence in comparison to success; but how anxious this makes us all!

10 P.M.

All has gone on well up to this time. The fog has cleared away, and the wind is now due east, but there is a heavy sea running and the old ship is rolling a little. I have been watching the cable leaving the tanks for some time this evening, and feel more comfortable at he work as now going on. We have reduced the speed of the ship to about 4½ knots, and I hope at that speed it will not be difficult for the men in the tank, particularly as we have increased their number to-day, to prevent any similar accident to the one we had last night.

Thursday, July 19th.

It is a week to-night since we lifted our anchor at Bearhaven. May I hope in another week we will be in sight of land on the other side. I will earnestly hope and pray it may be so. Our cable work has gone on very well since last night, and we were at noon to-day in lat. 51° 54' 30", long. 29° 39', or 713 miles on our way and 956 miles from the end of our journey, so that we have now got the distance into three figures. We made 112.2 miles since yesterday. I will not calculate the future. Our after tank will be finished to-night at about eleven o'clock, and we will change into the forward one. It is a delicate operation, but by stopping the ship, I hope it will be safely accomplished.

Friday, July 20th.

The cable in our aft tank was finished last night, and the forward tank was commenced at 11 P.M. The change was very well done by our men. The ship was stopped while the last ten or twelve coils were paid out. The weather was everything we could wish, calm and smooth sea. For some time before this the sky was overcast by clouds, but when I looked up into the sky after watching the operation, I saw the evening star shining in all its beauty—a happy omen, I hope, of the work to be done from the new tank. Oxford Street now looks very cheerful at night. We call the side of the ship where the cable runs Oxford Street. The whole length of the ship is lighted with large lamps about fifteen feet apart, and has quite the effect of a long street, and it is a good long one, being nearly one-eighth of a mile long. It was a great advantage to us having such fine weather to perform so difficult an operation. All my friends in England would be in bed, as we are now two hours and more behind London time. This morning the weather was very fine, and a ship and a whale were seen; but as I was not on deck, I had not the benefit of the excitement. The sound of the bells on the accompanying ships had a very pleasing sound. They were very close to us this morning, and we could hear them every half hour, like village bells in the distance. Towards twelve o'clock it began to rain and the wind gradually to rise, coming on also very cold. At one o'clock we were just half way across, and seven days from making the splice off Valencia. At noon we were in lat. 51° 36', long. 32° 47' 30", having run since yesterday 117.5 miles, and payed out 127.46 miles of cable. We were 830 miles from Valencia and 838 miles from Heart's Content. I should be glad to get a good night to-night, for the last three have been very bad ones, and I feel rather done up. I do not fancy I am as well this voyage as I was last; it may be fancy, but I certainly feel the anxiety more; it is never ceasing. I now hear the rumble of the cable over my head in my cabin, and am constantly listening to it. This stretch of the nerves day after day is hard work, and the mind has no change; morning, noon, and night it is all the same—cable, cable, cable. We get news every day from Valencia.

Saturday, July 21st.

We had a much better night last night than it promised. By midnight the gale had blown itself out, and this morning the sea gradually went down. It was some amusement to us to see our companions using a patent self-acting deck-washing machine, as they dipped their bows under the water and sent it along their decks, while we were going along as steady as a rock. During the forenoon we had some slight scuds of rain, but they blew off, and the day since has been beautifully fine. To-night is the first clear moon-light night we have had. All has gone on well with the cable. Early in the morning one of the flakes caught, but so slightly, there was no difficulty in checking it; yet it shows how necessary constant vigilance is, and how soon our hopes may be blighted. I think the feeling of confidence is rising in the ship. I hear them speaking of our landing at Heart's Content. I confess to something of the same feeling, but dare not indulge it. As I walked along the deck this morning, an old fellow, one of the men, overtook me, and looking up into my face, said, "I think we are going to do it this time, sir." Our telegrams from Valencia, I think, bring the matter before the minds of the men. We post them up written in large writing outside the electrical room, and there is generally a crowd round the board, some reading, others copying it down. I had a telegram this morning at breakfast, giving me the latest news of this morning, and Field wanted to telegraph to a person in Liverpool to ask if some information as to the Newfoundland telegraphs had arrived in Liverpool by the *Java*. The telegram was sent from here, one thousand miles from the land, at 9 A.M., and the answer from Liverpool came back at 2 P.M. Tonight we have a telegram giving us the news of the defeat of the Italian fleet by the Austrians. I have now been more than three weeks in the ship; it looks a long time. To-day we were in lat. 51° 18', long. 36° 1', having run 121.9 miles, and payed out 135.73 miles of cable. Our distance from Heart's Content is 716.7 miles. I remember well, as we passed over this ground last year, Canning and I, on an evening like the present, had a long walk on the deck, talking with perfect confidence of our arrival in Heart's Content, and the day following all our hopes were blighted. Tonight we have also had a long stroll, but we tempered our hopes with an "if," and looked forward to our western haven as something we might attain to, but not with certainty. God grant us our hopes may be realised.

Sunday, July 22nd.

A little before noon to-day we passed, about thirty-five miles to the south, the end of our lost cable. I looked to see if I could recognise the scenery in which we spent so many anxious hours; but the waves looked very like what we have been passing through now for some time; the only familiar thing in the scene was the old *Terrible*. At six o'clock we were over the deepest water in the whole distance, it being 2424 fathoms. We now gradually shallow as we go on. There has been a good deal of talking to-day about Heart's Content. I will wait a couple more days before I begin to paint any pictures of that happy land. I spent some time to-night in the electrical room watching the signals coming from Valencia. It is very beautiful to see the play of that little speck of light telling you the wishes of those who are sending it through 2300 miles of distance. Our position at noon to-day was lat. 50° 48', long. 39° 14', or 1075.7 miles from Valencia and 593.3 miles from Heart's Content. The amount of cable payed out has been 133.14 miles, and altogether 1207.47. There was a very beautiful sunset to-night. I hope the fine weather will continue, but the moon looks a little hazy and doubtful. How enjoyable a quiet day at Clewer would have been to-day! This is my fourth Sunday on board. If we go all right with this cable, I suppose in a fortnight I will be back on this same ground to try and get up the 1865 cable. Now for a walk in Oxford Street, and then to bed. Good night. Stars bright.

Monday, July 23rd.

This is the anniversary of our start from Valencia last year, and the beginning of many troubles. All has gone on well with us during the last twenty-four hours. The cable has continued to run over our stern in a quiet and regular manner. It often makes me wonder, when I go on deck, to see that same rope running that I have looked on now for so many days, continually on the move and working its way mile by mile down deep into the dark waters of the Atlantic, never to be seen more, yet full of life, and conveying the thoughts and wishes of man through all that mighty sea of waters.

A message was sent to-day and answer returned in eight minutes, the speed being four and a half words per minute. This through 2400 miles of cable, a large portion of which is in the coils of our tank, where the speed is much slower than it is when stretched out in a straight line. The calculations for distance reduced to the actual length of the cable when laid, or say 1900 miles, and allowing for the loss by the part in our coils, will give a speed of about eight words—a much better speed than it was considered possible, as we are using the old kind of instruments. If all goes well for another thirty-six hours, we will be out of danger and in shallow water.

Tuesday, July 24th.

Another day is gone, and one more will make us quite safe; we are now in 1500 fathoms of water, and by mid-day to-morrow it will be reduced to 500, in which we can have no difficulty in dealing with the cable. I am very weary to-night, and feel half ill. I got no sleep last night, for I had not been very long asleep when I woke up with the belief that the ship had stopped. I listened a little while, but could not be satisfied, so got up and looked out of my window at the paddles; they were going, but I thought slow. I tried to hear the cable running along the deck, but could not be sure. I then went to the grand saloon, and thought I heard the rumble of the pulleys, so again got into bed, but could not again sleep. Oh, what weary hours these hours of the night are when you have nothing to do but to paint pictures of misfortune! I was glad when a reasonable hour to get up arrived. I tried to paint pictures of happiness in England, recalled happy hours, but it was hard to keep my thoughts on anything but the cable. I then recalled the scene in the tank, and felt it must all go on well, but no sleep would give me a few hours of oblivion. In the daytime, when I am about and can watch the cable, I then feel confidence, but night is very hard. To-day all has gone on well; the weather, with the exception of a couple of hours in the middle of the day, has been a thick fog, and the steam-whistle has been regularly at work, but we have made our usual progress, being at noon in lat. 49° 45', long. 45° 21', and have run a distance of 122.7 miles and payed out 134.82 miles of cable. We are now 1319.6 miles on our journey and have 349.4 miles to go, so that if all goes well we will finish our work and land our cable on Friday. The forward tank is now just empty, and at eleven to-night we will change the middle tank. It will be my last walk in Oxford Street, as two-thirds of it will be cut off when we are paying out of the middle tank. This changeable Atlantic! When I sat down to write this I could see the moon out of my window through the fog, and it is now raining very hard; I hear it against my window. If it continues like this we will get a good wetting when it is time to go on deck and change tanks. Well, I will try and read for half-an-hour and then go on deck and see the change of tanks made, and will hope for some sleep afterwards.

Wednesday, July 25th.

Thank God, our cable is now safe; that is, we are certain to complete it, for now we are in shallow water, and if any accident did occur, we could without difficulty, and with very little loss of time, pick it up, our depth now being only about 700 fathoms. To-morrow early we will be in 170 fathoms, or where we can drop an anchor. What a relief this is to us all. It has been a hard fortnight; that is a long time to feel that from one minute to another you might be involved in misfortune. Those who are on shore, and get the information once a day, make up their minds that, for twenty-four hours they cannot hear anything more, and so are reconciled to the delay, but we could not feel certain for a moment. Well, it is over, and success in so great a work will amply reward us. All on board have certainly done their duty like Englishmen; they have never flagged in attention and zeal, nor could have behaved better; and I say this of all—ship's crew, cablemen, electricians, engineers—in fact, every department have thrown their whole heart into the work, and will greatly rejoice at the success. Long may they be spared in health and happiness to boast of it. We finished the forward tank last night about eleven o'clock, and commenced the middle. The change was made in a most satisfactory manner. The night was calm, but wet, and to-day we have had nothing but thick fog and heavy rain, the steam-whistles going all day. I hope we may have the next two days clear, to enable us comfortably and without delay to make our port. The *Albany* will go ahead the first thing in the morning to look out for the land, and for a Government ship that has been stationed about thirty-five miles from Heart's Content to guide us into the harbour; but if the fog is as thick as it is to-day, it will not be safe to take this large ship in. If all be well, we will land the shore-end on Friday, and see what kind of a place it is we are going to.

Thursday, July 26th.

How changed is our ship to-day; every one seems as though a heavy load of care and anxiety has been removed from his mind. We undoubtedly, for the last fortnight, have been a gloomy lot, almost afraid to smile or laugh, in case the next second might turn our laugh into crying.

We have achieved our great object and laid our cable from shore to shore, along which the lightning may now flash messages of peace and goodwill between two kindred nations. Is it wrong that I should have felt as though my heart would burst when that end of our long line touched the shore amid the booming of cannon, the wild half-mad cheers and shouts of the men? It seemed more than I could bear. How many anxious hours has the realisation of this day cost me; yet I am rewarded. I am given a never-dying thought "that I aided in laying the Atlantic cable." Future years may show that many have been laid, but the experience of the first, although it may and will make others less difficult, can never make the task a light one. It must ever be one of great risk, so little can destroy it. We have now to bend our thoughts and energies to picking up the old cable.

At four this morning I heard a gun fire, and went on deck, when I found there was a patch of land visible on our port side, but all around was fog. We were, however, in Trinity Bay, and could see the accompanying ships. By degrees, but very slowly, the fog cleared off and by seven o'clock we had it pretty clear, and then got a view of the land on each side. The outline of the hills is very pretty, but barren, that is, of cultivation; they are covered with a small, stunted fir, and some kind of undergrowth. Soon after nine we had got up to the place where we had fixed to begin the heavy shore-end. The paddle-box boats of the *Terrible* were sent to us to carry the end of the cable, and preparations were made to cut it off from the *Great Eastern*. This was all complete by ten o'clock, when it was cut, and the work of the *Great Eastern* was over. I left her and went on board the *Medway*; soon after which, the *Great Eastern,* turning round upon her centre by the united action of the screw and paddles, to the astonishment of all in the other vessels who saw the operation, put on steam and went majestically off to her anchorage in Heart's Content Bay. By this time the day was lovely and warm, with a nice bright sun and clear atmosphere. The end was then carried to the *Medway*, and the operation of making the splice to the shore-end was begun. This occupied about three hours, when we moved ahead, gradually paying out the heavy cable. All went out well, and we got as near the shore as we could—say 100 yards—and dropped our anchor. Canning and I then landed, to determine the best place to land the end. Having fixed upon this, the cable was coiled in one of the paddle-box boats, and assisted by some other ship's boats, it was slowly laid into its watery bed to the land. There then was the wildest excitement I had ever witnessed. All seemed mad with joy, jumping into the water and shouting as though they wished the sound to be heard at Washington. As soon as the cable touched the land a signal from the shore was made, and all the ships in the harbour fired a salute. I do not know how many guns were fired, but the noise was something tremendous, and the smoke soon hid the ships from our view. The reverberations of the sound of the guns amongst the hills round the bay was very grand. While the cable was being stored in the boats and coming on shore, we had employed a lot of the natives to cut the trench for it up to the little wooden house now used as a telegraph office. A very short time was needed to carry the end up to this house. As soon as it reached there, which it did at four (local time), another wild scene of excitement took place. The old cable hands seemed as though they could eat the end; one man actually put it into his mouth and sucked it. They held it up and danced round it, cheering at the top of their voices. It was a strange sight—nay, a sight that filled our eyes with tears. Yes, I felt not less than they did. I did cheer, but I could better have silently cried. Well, it is a feeling that will last my life; it will be one of those thoughts which will assist to bring peace to my mind when other matters trouble it. I am glad two of my boys were present to enjoy and glory in their part of so noble a work. They may, long after I am gone, tell their children of what we did. Steps were now taken to couple the end with the instruments in the house, and get ready for work. While this was being done, we all went to the little wooden church in the village, the clergyman having offered to perform the service. There were three clergymen assembled to see the cable, and all took part in the service, which was very nicely done, the clergyman of the village reading the prayers, a couple of hymns were sung, and we all earnestly returned our thanks to God in the words of the thanks giving in the Prayer Book, "Particularly to those who desire to offer up their praises and thanksgiving for Thy late mercies vouchsafed to them in the performance of the great work they have just completed." After church was over, I then had the first telegram sent through the cable from shore to shore. It was as follows:—

"Mr. Gooch, Heart's Content, to Mr. Glass, Valencia,
July 27th, 6 P.M.

"Our shore-end has just been laid, and a most perfect cable, under God's blessing, has completed telegraphic communication between England and the continent of America.

"I cannot find words fully to express my deep sense of the untiring zeal and the earnest and cheerful manner in which every one on board, from the highest to the lowest, has performed the anxious and arduous duties they in their several departments have had to perform; their untiring energy, and able and watchful care, night and day, for a period of two weeks, required to complete this work, can only be fully understood and appreciated by one who like myself has seen it. All have faithfully done their duty and glory in their success, and heartily join with me in congratulations to our friends in England who have also laboured in carrying out this great work."

I felt the first words our child ought to speak was to express to those engaged in its birth its thanks for their able aid; and, indeed, all have well done their duty. The second message through the cable was as follows:—

"D. Gooch, Heart's Content, to Lord Stanley,[2] Foreign Office, Whitehall, London, July 27th, 6.30 P.M.
"Mr. Gooch has the pleasure to inform Lord Stanley that the Newfoundland shore-end of the Atlantic cable was laid to-day, and the most perfect telegraphic communication established between England and the continent of America. God grant it may be a lasting source of great benefit to our country. The message of Her Majesty to the President of the United States has been received, and I hope the arrangements for communicating across the Gulf of St. Lawrence will be completed by Monday, when the message will be at once forwarded."

This message reached me at breakfast time this morning. It is to the following effect:—

"Lord Stanley requests that the following message may be forwarded immediately:—

"The Queen, Osborne, to the President of the United States, Washington.
"The Queen congratulates the President on the successful completion of an undertaking which she hopes may serve as an additional bond of union between the United States and England."

As our success is now known in England, I feel there will be many kind hearts that will rejoice with me. How I wish I could pass over by telegraph, and receive their congratulations and see their pleasure. Well, that day will come after we have done something more for fame, and picked up the cable of 1865. In the meantime I will picture to myself all I know I would receive if I could be there now, and will now conclude a feeble description of a red letter day in my life.

Saturday, July 28th.

The leader of the *Times* on the cable, of which an extract was sent, says, "It is a great work, a glory to our age and nation, and the men who have achieved it deserve to be honoured among the benefactors of their race."

Walking along the deck after this was posted on our news board, some sailors had stopped to read it; one of them after doing so said to the other, "I say, Bill, we be benefactors to our race." "Yes," says Bill, "we be," and he strutted along with his back straight and his head at least two inches higher.

HEART'S CONTENT, *Wednesday, August 1st.*

It must be awfully solitary work living in such a place, with only a few acres cleared around you, and all the rest wild mountain and wood. We got a few white roses, almost the only flowers in what they call a garden, and there was only one tree of this. We got back to the ship for dinner after a pleasant walk, as the weather on our return had cleared up, and was at any rate dry.

Friday, August 3rd.

A telegram was sent through the cable to-day coming from Vancouver's Island, a distance of 6000 miles. All is working well, and I am getting very impatient of our delay here. I want to get off to the fishing ground and get up the old cable, so that we may return to England. It is five weeks to-day since I came to the ship, a long time, and I fear it will be in any case nearly a month before I get back.

Saturday, August 4th.

This has been a lovely day, and we have had a strong party on board. I suppose some twenty-four or twenty-five ladies have been here, and ten or twelve of them are sleeping on board—a pretty noise they are making with their dancing and singing. I hope they will not forget it is Saturday night, and let me get to sleep by twelve o'clock.

The work on the cable is going on very well. Yesterday we had fifty messages, paying us, I suppose, not less than £1200. This will do as a start, as it is equal to between £300,000 and £400,000 a year. If we only had the line open direct to America, it will, I have no doubt, increase very much; the delay now sadly interferes with the receipts.

BACK IN THE ATLANTIC, *Thursday, August 9th.*

We got our anchor up at twelve o'clock, and began to move out of the harbour at 12.10. I hope to return to it in ten or twelve days with cable No. 2. I trust this will be done, and have great confidence it will be. May God grant us success. I am in hopes, when we reach the broken end on Sunday, we will find the *Terrible* and the *Albany* have got a buoy on the cable; if so, our delay there will not be long. The *Medway* is steaming close to us. We got rid of all our party out of the ship at about nine o'clock, and right glad was I to see the ship cleared and the last boatload go off to the *Lily.* We breakfasted at seven o'clock, so as to get them away early, and we had hoped to start by ten, but the chains of the anchors got twisted, and it took some time to get them cleared. It was a lovely morning, and very hot until we got out of the harbour of Heart's Content, when some heavy rain came on, and it has been cooler since. How strange it is to part and say good-bye to people you have been seeing frequently for a couple of weeks, and with whom you have got up a kind of friendship, knowing well there is no chance of your ever meeting again, that your good-bye is a final one. It was so with two or three we saw this morning for the last time. They have shown us all the kindness and hospitality in their power. The *Lily* left at the same time we did, and goes direct to St. John's. Our ship is drawing 26 feet forward and 32 feet aft, so that she is a couple of feet too deep by the stern for good trim, but we have been making about nine knots per hour. I got my last news from England just as we were starting, so that at twelve o'clock here I had the prices and London news up to twelve o'clock there. It will be some days before we may hear anything new, but if we get up the broken cable we will then be in communication with Valencia again. I can fancy how glad some of my friends will be if they hear, as they will at once, should we get hold of that old end we lost twelve months ago, and thus make our summer's work complete, and it will be very complete, and content me with the work of cable-laying. I can then with satisfaction give it up to younger hands.

Saturday, August 11th.

Twelve months ago to-day we left our fishing ground and returned to England. To-morrow we will be on the same spot, and for the same object. We are now anxiously looking forward to meeting the *Albany* and *Terrible*, and learning what they have done towards picking up the cable. I fancy we will reach them about two o'clock to-morrow, and then we will get a very good notion of our chance of success. It rained very hard all last night, and did not clear up until between nine and ten this morning, when it gradually up to mid-day brightened, and enabled an observation to be taken at twelve. We were then in lat. 50° 12', long. 44° 40', and had done 192 miles since yesterday. We are not making the speed I hoped we would. Since mid-day to-day a strong wind has sprung up, and we have put some sail on the ship. This may help us a little. The sea has become very angry, and it is a fine sight to stand on the paddle-box and see it striking on the side of the ship, and then bounding off again in a mass of white foam, the wind carrying the spray some distance, but the whole surface of the sea is covered with white foam, and the notion is it will blow harder during the night. I am glad now of anything that saves time, and as the wind is in our favour, the harder it blows the better for my task. I find the days get very long, and I long to see the end of our voyage. There is now nothing to interest one, and walking the deck and reading all day becomes very monotonous and wearying. We saw a full-rigged ship to-night in the distance. The *Medway* is showing plenty of life. Charlie is on board of her, and I fancy is wishing himself back in the *Great Eastern* to-night. The night is cloudy and the stars not visible, and I am going to bed at 9.30 to have a quiet read, if I do not go to sleep. Every one in the ship was complaining yesterday of not feeling well—some were in bad spirits, some had headache, and all were weary and sleepy. I certainly felt the latter very strongly, and have to-day had a heavy feel, but no headache. We do not get any telegrams now, and do not know what is going on in the world, but in a few days, if we have good luck, we will be able to converse again through our cable.

Sunday, August 12th.

Here we are once more in our old fishing ground, lat. 51° 26', long. 38° 57', and a nice time we have had of it the last twenty-four hours. The old ship has been trying to show us what she can do in the way of rolling, and has given us the benefit. The wind and sea got up late last night from the south-west, and I soon found it was impossible to sleep. I was rolled from one side of my bed to the other like a rolling pin, and heard first one thing and then another tumble down on the floor. When I went on deck the sea was very grand. As I looked over it I could imagine lines of mountains capped with snow, and the boiling and surging of the waves against the side of the ship was grand in the extreme. Several times they dashed up the side, and the wind catching the top, carried the spray of water right across the ship. The *Medway*, although not a quarter of a mile from us, was often hidden from our sight, even when standing on the top of our high paddle-box. Often the waves came rushing upon us, their tops higher than our decks, as though they intended to swallow us up. It is an awful scene, these angry waters of the Atlantic, and our old ship rolled about in them as though she was a cork, instead of the mighty mass she is. She rolled pretty regularly about 36°, making about five rolls per minute. We have been obliged to have the fiddles on the tables all day, and at lunch my chair began a rapid slide across the cabin, leaving me on my hands and knees on the floor. The day has been fine, with scuds of fine rain, and as the wind has changed, the sea is going down, so I hope we will have a better night, and a fine day for our work to-morrow. We came in sight of the *Albany* at two o'clock, and soon after saw the *Terrible*. Our captain had steered for them well, as they were right ahead in our course. At three we came up to the *Albany,* and one of the buoys she had put down at about a mile and a half from the end of the cable. She told us by signal she had put another down about fifteen miles to the east. She also told us she had hooked and raised the cable about 150 fathoms, when the chain some

30 yards from the grapnel had broken, but I think there must be some mistake in the signal. The sea was too high to go very near her. She was uncommonly lively. I should not have liked to be in either her or the *Medway*. As soon as we came up to her we slowed speed, and got the ship's head round to the wind, which relieved our rolling very much, and we are now steering very slowly ahead with the wind; intending to do so until about midnight, when we will turn round and return to the buoy, hoping then to be able to make arrangements for getting hold of the cable. A couple of fine days will, I believe, enable us to get it on board. I cannot see any good reason why we should not do so. We ran 206 miles up to twelve to-day, and were then in lat. 51° 26', and long. 39° 40'. It is pleasant to be able to get a good night's rest, so good night. No stars, but a small rain.

Monday, August 13th.

We have had a nice change in the weather to-day, and a very calm sea, but I fear have not done much good towards getting the end of the cable. We had all the early part of the day a nice breeze for drifting across the cable from the north, but our grapnel was not lowered until one o'clock, by which time the wind had died away, and we have made no progress towards the cable, a current in the water being fully a balance for the power of the wind. Now we are hauling in our grapnel again, intending to go to the south of the cable, and take advantage of the current and any southerly wind, which the captain says we are sure to have next. I admit I feel some disappointment at this day being lost; the weather has been so fine, one cannot but regret the loss of a whole day.

Tuesday, August 14th.

There is a better prospect to-night of fine weather, and the men learned in nautical matters say the wind will go down, and we will have a fine day to-morrow. All is ready to let go the grapnel at daylight if the weather suits.

Wednesday, August 15th.

During last night it came on a heavy fog, and when I got up this morning, instead of finding, as I hoped, our grapnel down, we could scarcely see the length of the ship, and of course did not know where we were, nor any of our friends. A little after eight it began to rain very heavily, and this continued until eleven, when the fog had cleared away, and we found ourselves within sight of No.1 buoy, and the other ships not far from us. As the wind was the way we wanted, it was determined to make a trial with the grapnel, and we steamed away a few miles to the south of the cable, and at 12.30 began to lower it. This was completed by about a quarter to two. The *Medway* was sent a couple of miles to the west to lower her grapnel also. Soon after this was done the fog came on again, and has shut us in ever since; although there was blue sky and sun overhead, a heavy bank of fog rested on the water, and a very wet fog it has been, one's clothes get covered with it like hoar-frost. Most of the afternoon I have been watching the dynamometer. We calculated that at the estimated drift of the ship we would be on the line of cable about six o'clock. Soon after six, when we were at dinner, an officer came down to say the strain on the dynamometer had increased, so we all hoped the cable was hooked. The line is so heavy it is difficult to know when the cable is on, but the drift of the ship stopped as though she was anchored. After much discussion, it was finally settled to begin to haul up. This we did at eight o'clock; and it is now slowly coming in, with strong indications that we have the cable. In a short time the matter will be certain. We put down 2200 fathoms of line, and are raising it at the rate of half-a-mile per hour, the strain on the dynamometer being about 10 tons.

Thursday, August 16th, 11 A.M.

When I went on deck again last night I found the line had been hauled in to 1600 fathoms, with a steady strain of about 11 tons, giving clear indications that we had lifted the cable about 350 fathoms from the bottom. After much discussion, it was then deemed better, although I did not think so, to buoy it in that position. Steps were at once taken to do this. While this was being done, we found No.1 buoy close to our starboard paddle, and it soon got under our sponson, and began to thump the ship very hard. After much difficulty it was got clear, but, as we discovered this morning, at the expense of the buoy, as it is nowhere visible, and has no doubt had a hole broken into it, and has sunk. At one o'clock all was ready to let down the buoy to hold the cable, but on the line out, the splice of the eye pulled out, and over it went, losing not only our day's work, but 1600 fathoms of line. This splice must have been very badly made, or it would not have given way as it did. This is very disheartening, this being the second buoy line that we have lost, to say nothing of the time. Nothing more, however, could be done, and this morning we steamed to the *Medway*, as she had let down a grapnel yesterday afternoon. We have just learned from her that she has not hooked the cable, and is now lifting her grapnel, and we have settled to steam off to buoy No.4, and collect the ships there, with the intention of all three driving across the cable, and taking a joint pull at it.

9.30 P.M.

We steamed to buoy No. 4, and the *Albany* and *Medway* joined us there. It was then arranged that we should each take a line to the east of this buoy, about two and a half miles apart, and so cross the cable, and see which of us first picked it up. We began to lower our grapnel at two o'clock, and have been drifting slowly, assisted by the starboard paddle, the other being disconnected, and about half-an-hour ago the strain on the dynamometer began to increase, and we have begun to haul in. We had just concluded we had missed the cable, and orders had been given to take up the grapnel, with the view of going back to our old position and trying again. A short time will show whether we have anything or not. I am getting very weary of this life, and shall be sincerely glad when it is over, yet I cannot help hoping we may be able to get the old cable on deck. I daresay if we do so I will forget my disgust with the work.

Friday, August 17*th,* 11 A.M.

It is very, very hard and sad to hear, after a morning of the most extreme anxiety, we have just had a sadly bitter disappointment. After hauling upon our grapnel last night for a short time we were satisfied we had hooked the cable, and after lifting it about 100 fathoms from the bottom, it was thought better to let the ship hang to it until daylight this morning, as there was no wind. Lifting commenced again this morning, and we gradually got up our line, all the indications proving we were lifting the cable, and at 10.30 our chain and grapnel came to the surface with the cable on it, the cable being hooked on two of the prongs of the grapnel, and stretching out at a considerable angle east and west. The boats of the *Terrible* had come to our bows to assist in putting on the stoppers. When the cable came up the whole ship resounded with cheers, but how short was our joy; just as they were putting on the stoppers, and not five minutes after we had raised it, snap it went, and down went our joy and our heart also. God knows it was a bitter feeling, and is enough to dishearten us. The weather, although wet for an hour between eight and nine o'clock, is all we wish, and the sea has gone down very much. Well, we must not despair; the *Albany* is lifting it about two and a half miles to the east of us, and the *Medway*, having missed it last night, has let down her grapnel an hour and a half ago, and I hope one of them will get it up. And as we now have a broken end, at a place we know well, we will have less strain on the next lifts, and will then hope to get it on board; but only to lift it and look on our old line again for a few minutes, and then to see it once more drop into the depths of the ocean, requires some philosophy to bear with fortitude.

We have got a new noise in the ship the last two nights. As the paddle-engines are not working, the seas move them a little, and in doing this the outside bearing on the port side bellows like a great bull, and you could fancy the same animal was at your bed-head in a towering passion. This is not conducive to sleep, but practice is now making one tolerably independent of noises, and it did not prevent my having a very happy dream last night.

Friday, 10 P.M.

The result of a day's talking and a morning's experience is that we can with certainty recover the cable, but we must have patience and wait for the weather, which has been sadly against us all the time we have been out this year. We have now made a new end, free from all the ropes that have been lost. I do not know whether I mentioned that the *Medway* a couple of days ago, when she hauled in her grapnel, found it broken and bent as though it had passed over rocks; the line was also worn into the wires; she must have passed over a very rough bottom. The old cable we lifted to-day shows that it had sunk a very short way into the mud, for one side of it was white, as though coated with the ooze, the other half black as we laid it down last year. Whether the oozy side was down or up we don't know, but at any rate only half the cable had been buried. When the cable was hanging on the grapnel it was very much chafed, and thereby weakened. It was settled at noon to take a new position and try again. The *Medway* was sent about two and a half miles to the east to grapnel also, and by two o'clock our grapnel was again down, but after a little it was found that both the wind and the set of the current had varied, and we could not drift across the cable. The weather had also changed very much for the worse, a high wind with rain, and a heavy, broken sea, getting up; so the grapnel was again lifted, and got in a little before six. We then went to the *Medway*, and found her drift was as useless as ours, and she was ordered to haul up her grapnel, and, like ourselves, make themselves as comfortable as they can for the night, and until a change of weather; so here we are all in a heap, keeping as near No. 4 buoy as we can without fouling each other.

Saturday, August 18th.

Since last night up to mid-day to-day the weather has been very bad, and we have been shifting about to find our buoy. The wind is still very rough, now two o'clock, but the sun has come out, and I have just heard that the *Terrible* has found the buoy, so I suppose we will be off to her and take our chance of getting our grapnel down if the wind goes down at sunset. It blows very cold from the east, and as the deck is so uncomfortable, it is very hard to get through the time, and we all groan in spirit.

10 P.M.

The lost buoy has been discovered, but the flagstaff and ball had been broken off, hence the great difficulty in seeing it. Another buoy was put down from this ship about six miles east of it, and as the weather has cleared up and the wind and sea very much gone down this afternoon, there is some hopes we may be able to get the grapnel down in the morning. The better the day the better the deed, although Friday has got a good name as the cable day, for we made our splice on a Friday, landed at Heart's Content on a Friday, and raised the old cable to the surface on a Friday. If we have the good fortune to bring it on board to-morrow, we will land the second cable on a Friday. I only hope it is not to be our fate to wait here until next Friday.

Sunday, August 19*th.*

This morning at eight o'clock we lowered our grapnel, the sea being tolerably smooth and other things being favourable, and we slowly drifted all day to find the cable; this we succeeded in doing at four o'clock this afternoon, and at once began to haul up. By six we had hauled 1200 fathoms, and it was then determined to buoy it, and get it up by degrees at another lift. The *Albany* has hooked it about a mile south of us, and has hauled in 936 fathoms. She has now orders to hang on as she is until the morning. How far this may succeed is uncertain, as she has just telegraphed us that her grapnel is sliding along the cable towards us with a strain of only four tons. We have 8 tons on. The operation of buoying is rather a hazardous one, but greater care is being taken to-night with the splice at the eye than was done last time, and I hope it will go all right; but it will be an hour yet before it is ready to place the buoy on board. The night is not so dark as we have had it, although it is cloudy; yet the clouds are thin, and the moon is giving a good light through them. A fine day to-morrow is all important to us, as, if we are to have any assistance from the other ships, they are no use except in calm weather. The *Medway* has been away between two and three miles to the east, but we do not know yet that she has got hold of the cable. We fancy not. There has been a strong breeze all day, making a short, broken sea, and the heavy swell has quite gone down.

Monday, August 20*th.*

Oh that we could secure twenty-four hours of calm weather! We would then, I think, be certain of the cable. We managed to get it safely buoyed last night between ten and eleven o'clock, the cable being one thousand fathoms from the ground. It was fortunate we settled to do this, as the wind and sea to-day have both been too heavy to have enabled us with safety to get the end on board. The weather has not been so cold to-day as it was yesterday, for it was then bitterly cold—quite a greatcoat day. The sun has been shining most of to-day, and a good observation has been taken of our buoy, to which the bight of the cable is hanging. It is in lat. 51° 31' 30", long. 38° 39' 50", and about six miles from the end we broke on Friday last.

Tuesday, August 21*st.*

We have been again disappointed in the weather, and have not been able to make any progress with our work. Here we lay, steaming a little, and then allowing the ship to drift back again, rolling about like a useless log on the ocean. It is a sad loss of time, and makes one very impatient. I was in great hopes from the look of things last night. that we would have had a calm day to-day. The day has been very fine overhead, and the wind has changed to the north. This has reduced the sea very much, and I think since mid-day the wind has gone down a good deal; but I have just been on deck, and it is a cold and cheerless night, very cloudy, so that we see no moon. The evening star was, however, very bright, shining through a small opening in the clouds. We had a little excitement this morning; No. 4 buoy was found to be adrift, and we went to pick it up. It was no easy task for the sailor who had to go down to it and hook on the block. The sea kept thumping it about, and as he got on to it, it turned round and let him into the water. He had plenty of pluck, and succeeded at last in getting the hook fast, but I was very much afraid he might get killed between the buoy and the side of the ship, as it hit us pretty hard blows. The excitement lasted half-an-hour, and this was something to break the monotony of the day. The chain had chafed through at the ring under the buoy, and so lost us upwards of two miles of buoy-line. The bottom of the Atlantic here will be paved with rope, as we lost about six miles of it last year. It certainly is the most unfortunate part of the Atlantic for us to have to perform this lifting operation, as it is notoriously the worst part for weather.

Wednesday, August 22nd.

This has been a day of much disappointment; the weather and the sea have been, if not calm, yet moderate, yet we have failed to make any progress. Much time was lost the first thing in the morning in arranging the programme with the other ships. The *Medway* was then sent towards the west to grapple, the *Albany* to the east, and the *Great Eastern* was to cross the cable a short distance to the east of the bight buoy. It was some time before the other ships had taken up their positions and lowered their grapnels, and as we waited for them to get hold of the cable first, it was 11.30 before we began to lower our grapnel. When it was down, we saw the *Albany* coming back to us to say the sea was too heavy for her to grapnel, as the pitching strained the line, so she gave up. We then soon found that the *Great Eastern* would not drift in the direction we wanted her; the currents here seem to change their direction every hour in the day. One of the paddles was disconnected, but nothing would do, and by four o'clock all attempt to get her across the cable at the place that would be of any use to us was found useless, and we began to heave up. The *Medway* had by this time signalled to us to say she had the cable. We then hoped, as it was near the end, she would get it to the surface and might be able to buoy it, so that we could take hold of it the first thing in the morning, but at five o'clock she signalled she had lost it, and so here we are just as we were several days ago, not a bit advanced, as far as I can see, in any way, and I begin to get very tired of it. At dinner to-day we were anything but jolly; a sense of failure seemed to hang upon every one's mind, although no one will admit of any doubt of success. I hear remarks, "Oh, we must stay here till Christmas rather than fail." But this is simple nonsense; if we cannot do it now, no length of time will enable us to do so. We are nearly the end of August, and bad weather will be the ruling feature in this part of the Atlantic. We are not likely to have any weather better than we have had, and are certain to have it much worse,—most likely bad enough to carry away all our buoys. Another of them was found to-day to be adrift, and was picked up by the *Albany*. I am quite willing to hope and try for a few days more; but then it will be time to go home if we have not got the cable.

Thursday, August 23rd.

A fortnight has passed away since we left Heart's Content, and we are still without our cable. It was hoped the *Medway* had hooked it last night, but we found at seven this morning that she had not done so. In fact, these small ships dance about so, that it is impossible to tell when they have the cable on the grapnel or not; they are, indeed, a useless expense to us. When it was found she had nothing on her grapnel, the *Great Eastern* took up a position to drift across the cable a mile and a half east of the bight buoy, the *Medway* was sent a couple of miles east of this, and our grapnel was lowered at about nine o'clock. The weather was fine, that is, the, sea had gone down very much, and was calmer than we have had it since coming here. There was also very little wind, and we hoped to make a good haul; but we soon found the current was against us, but by disconnecting the starboard paddle the captain managed to drive her astern slowly, in the direction we wished to go. All day we have had no end of anxiety. First she would not go the right way, then she would, and we might expect to hook the cable at twelve o'clock. Twelve o'clock came, and little progress had been made. Four o'clock came, and no cable, and we kept on doing our best by the aid of steam to drive her on the course until nearly seven o'clock, when it was clear we were past the cable, and orders were given to begin to haul in. This is now going on, and nearly completed. It may be the grapnel is foul of the chain; we had a case of this kind last year. Last night when the grapnel came up there was a piece of stone fast in the grapnel-spring about six inches long by three broad, and an inch thick, very much like granite in appearance, but I do not think it is granite.

Friday, August 24th.

I think when I left off writing last night we were hauling in the grapnel; it came up all right, and must either have jumped over the cable or we had not drifted far enough. The water is deeper here than where we have been grapnelling before, and as the same length of line was out, or 2800 fathoms, it may be that it was lifted off the ground, although I can hardly think so, as the depth is not 2100 fathoms. The *Terrible* is getting short of provisions, and sent to try and get some from us, but we cannot spare any. We killed our first ox to-day, but when once we begin upon them they do not last long. Our poultry are nearly all gone, and our sheep and pigs are rapidly declining in number. How I long to be back to dear friends in England and look again on my pretty house at Clewer! It is now some time since I heard anything from them. God grant them all every blessing. Good-night.

Saturday, August 25th.

Another day of great disappointment. During last night the wind and sea went down, and gave a good prospect of a very successful day's fishing; and at six this morning our grapnel was lowered, but in doing so the line showed itself so much injured by previous work from kinks and the unwinding of the rope, that after a couple of hundred fathoms had been paid out, it was considered better to haul it back and use another line. This was done, and it was not until ten o'clock that they were ready to lower again. The ship at the time was drifting in the right direction. As soon as the grapnel was on the ground the ship took it into her head to change the direction of her drift and go exactly the way she was not wanted; the starboard paddle was disconnected and sail set to see if she could be forced in the direction required; but all without effect, and it was found necessary to lift up the grapnel again, which was done about one o'clock. The *Medway* had also had her grapnel down to drift in the same way we expected it to do, but was equally unsuccessful, and she had also to haul it up. As we have none of the largest buoys on board, it was determined to get one from the *Albany*, in case we might need one at our next work, and some time was occupied in getting this from the *Albany* to our deck. This was not finished until nearly four o'clock, when we steamed to the south to take a drifting position in accordance with our experience of the morning, the *Albany* and *Medway* doing the same at about two miles apart, and soon after five we began to lower our grapnel. The evening is all that could be desired, a quiet sea and quite calm, and the drift so far taking us in the right direction. If we fail to-night I do not see what hopes we can have.

Sunday, August 26th.

Well, I left off last night with hopes that before morning we might be able to say we had made some advance in our work; the grapnel was down, and the night all we could wish as to weather. The ship drifted steadily in the direction we wanted, and soon after two this morning the strain on the dynamometer began to increase, and went up to 10½ tons. It was then considered the cable had been hooked, but after a quarter of an hour the strain suddenly fell to its line-strain of 7½ tons, showing us we had either broken the cable or had never had it. Orders were given to draw it up, and the grapnel came on board soon after eight o'clock this morning. The springs were all flattened against the shank, and the chain and grapnel were nearly polished bright, and came up without any ooze on it, showing that it had been dragging upon a gravel-bottom, and probably the strain was caused by some large stone catching the grapnel; at any rate we had not

got the cable, and our time was lost. The *Medway* signalled
to us that she had hooked it on the west of the bight buoy,
and had lifted it six hundred fathoms from the bottom, and
was then hanging on to it until she had orders what to do.
She was told to stay as she was, and it was settled for us to go
up to her and hook the cable a little to the west of her. When
we got up to her we found she was not more than half-a-
mile from the bight buoy; she had drifted along the line of
cable. We got up to her about 11 A.M, and having learned
the position, we steamed away to the south to let down our
grapnel. Very much delay occurred in getting this done; it
was 1.30 before they began to lower it, and 3.30 before it was
down. The drift of the ship was then found to be too much
to the west, and so that we would pass the end; it was then
attempted to drive her across the line of cable to the east
of the buoy, which succeeded better; but by this time we
saw the *Medway* coming towards us, and about five o'clock
she came and told us that at about twelve o'clock, on the
occasion of the ship taking a great pitch, when she rose with
the sea, the strain had fallen on her dynamometer from 7½
to less than 5, and she had either broken the cable or her
grapnel had become unhooked. It had no springs to it to
prevent its getting off. So here we were with all our time lost;
and what is worse, the bight buoy had changed its position
three miles, so that it is either free from the cable or else the
end made by the *Medway* has allowed it to drift this much.

Monday morning, August 27th, 10 A.M.
At about two o'clock this morning I was awoke by the
captain knocking at my door to tell me the *Medway* has just
passed our bow, firing a gun and giving three cheers that
the *Albany* had hooked the end of the cable, and lifted it
on board and buoyed it. This was good news, and spoilt the

rest of my night's rest, for which I did not complain. I got up early, and went on deck at seven. Temple came on board from the *Albany* with a piece of the cable he had cut off at the bight; it had come in with a strain of three tons. This corresponds with the strain we had last year. There is clearly a short loose end, as the cable had twisted itself like a rope, and the grapnel could only be released by cutting off the bight. All the flukes of the grapnel were bent out straight, and it was only the twisting of the cable that made it hold. The piece of cable brought on board is as perfect as the day it was laid down, the wires being quite free from rust. It had chafed a little on the grapnel. Now, although we have got an end to work upon, I will not let my mind jump to the conclusion that our task is over; it may be we have only some of the cable broken off by the hauls we have had, and that we are not in possession of the end of the sound cable in connection with Valencia. It will be very hard on us if this is so. God grant we are right. The weather is all we could wish—at least it is much better than anything we have had.

Monday night.

When I went on deck I found efforts were being made to tack the stern of the ship up to the buoy, and the boats were rowing to it with lines for the purpose of making fast to it. The wind had then freshened a good deal, and all the captain could do he could not get her to back as he wanted. Efforts were continually made to do so, and we had talked ourselves into stirring hopes and calculations of the day we would reach Heart's Content and be in England. Soon after twelve Moriarty, who had got a good observation at twelve o'clock, came aft with a long face to tell us the ship was nearly twelve miles out of her proper position, and that the buoys were also as much wrong. Now, this was an awful damper on our hopes, as it could only be accounted for by the cable we had got hold of being a loose piece, and all had drifted together to the north-east. As there seemed little chance of our getting the stern of the ship to pick up the cable, her head was steamed up to it and the lines without difficulty made fast. When we began to haul in, the cable came up double twisted together for about half-a-mile, when it came single, and after getting in nearly two miles the other end came in. Now, this was a pleasant end to all our hopes! However, there was no help for it, we must begin again. The first end that came in had no doubt been broken last year, as it was old; the last end was a fresh break. If we get no other comfort out of this disappointment, we have the satisfaction of seeing what perfect order the cable is in—just as it was laid down, even the tar on its surface being good; indeed, if a piece of old and a piece of new were laid down together no one could tell the difference. This proves the great durability of the cable when once laid.

Tuesday, August 28th.

This has been the finest day we have had. Indeed all have allowed we could not wish for anything better. A bright sun with a S.W. wind, warm and comfortable; a calm sea. Orders were given last night for all the ships to make during the night for the single buoy. We had done this, so that on finding it we might take our start from it this morning and begin another haul. So this morning we were all there, and a position for this ship taken up, and by nine o'clock our grapnel began to go down. The frequent use of our lines is making them very bad, and it was nearly twelve o'clock before we got it down. When Moriarty got his observation at twelve o'clock, he found the buoy had drifted from its old position seventeen miles to the east, and what we had done was no use. Now, if this would not try the patience of a saint, I don't know what would! There was nothing for it but to begin pulling up again, and take a new position now we know exactly where we are. So we had a mark buoy lowered, and orders were given for the ship to steam to the place we thought we had been at. I am so sick of this work, I have insisted upon giving up the attempt in this deep water and going back about ninety miles east, where it is only 1650 fathoms. Twenty-five per cent. of gain in depth is a very important one, and, in my opinion, with the weather we are now pretty sure to have, is our only chance. We cannot get twelve hours of really suitable weather, and without it our efforts are only so much waste exertion. I am glad to say our ship's head is now turned to the east, and we are making the best of our way to the shallow water. It is fortunate that on the 1st of August last year we had a capital observation at this place, and can therefore go with certainty to the spot.

Friday, August 31st.

Nothing could be better for our work than the weather to-day. It has been quite calm, and what little wind there was has been in the direction best for us. There was until mid-day a very heavy swell. As soon as it was possible to make certain by observation that the buoy we put down last night had not shifted, we steamed to a position so as to drift across the line of the cable in a south-eastern direction, and began to lower our grapnel at 10.30; but owing to the frequent stoppages from the bad state our lines are getting into, we did not get it down until 12.30, the depth being about 1900 fathoms. The *Medway* was sent a couple of miles to the west to lower her grapnel. This she did about 11 A.M. in 1950 fathoms. I wish we had been eight or nine miles farther to the east, where the depth is only 1650 fathoms, as we might as well have taken advantage of the shallowest known part. Since the grapnels were down both ships have been drifting very slowly in the right direction, and we hope to hook the cable between ten and eleven to-night. If we fail to-night in hooking it and to-morrow in getting it up, I shall certainly lose all hope of doing so at all. We have no excuse to-day as to the weather, and I hope it will keep fine over to-morrow.

Saturday, September 1st, 9 P.M.

All at the present moment looks as like success as it is possible for anything to do. I mentioned last night that our grapnel was down. We drifted very slowly until four o'clock, when the strain increased a little, and we then began to heave up. An hour or so afterwards the *Medway* signalled that she had also got the cable. We kept on heaving up at the rate of about 400 fathoms per hour until we raised the cable about 600 fathoms from the ground, the strain being nearly a ton more than the usual strain, so we have been speculating whether we have also got hold of the cable of 1858, which is close to us here. Having found the *Medway* was lifting all right, we stopped our engine, so as to enable her to get ahead of us and to break the cable at her grapnel. This she is now doing. As soon as we find she is a good way ahead of us we will go on, and, I hope, be able to get the cable safely on board. The weather is and has been all we could wish—no wind and a calm sea. There is a slight swell, but not enough to interfere with our operations. Everything, certainly, is as favourable just now as we could ask for. It is a lovely night, and the sea looks like a lake.

Sunday, September 2nd, 11 A.M

We have indeed achieved a glorious victory. What will they now say in England—those who told me so often I was mad to hope to recover last year's cable from the deep Atlantic? Under God's blessing we have recovered it, and are now steering for Heart's Content with a cable over our stern to complete the work we left unfinished last year. How I have thought of this hour, how I have longed for it, and what sacrifices I have made to obtain its accomplishment! Yet have not the feelings of the past few hours amply repaid me? Does not the weary anxiety of the last three weeks pale before the glorious feelings of to-day? It has been indeed three weeks of weary disappointment and harassing suspense, until our task became almost hopeless. We never could get suitable weather, and when we did, it lasted only for a few hours; but the last two days have been all we could wish for, and I felt we were casting our last die: if we failed in such weather, hope indeed would become extinct. I feel now very glad I persevered in carrying my point of changing our ground and coming back where we did. We had less depth of water, and at the old place the cable had been so much pulled about with the grapnels it was impossible to say where it lay, and, if we got it, whether it might not be like the last, only a short piece. We have been just three weeks to-day on the fishing-ground, and have put down thirteen buoys and recovered all but one. We have had the grapnels down in all thirty-two times, hooked the cable ten times, and buoyed it four times. Our lines have begun to get very bad, and it took nearly as long to lower the grapnel as to get it in.

But to return to our proceedings here last night. When I went on deck a little before ten o'clock, I found that the *Medway* had signalled that she had broken the cable when between 300 and 400 fathoms from the top. This was just what we wished her to do, as it then gave us a loose end to the west and relieved the strain on our bight. We were then hauling in slowly, the ship drifting slowly towards the east, and so giving us slack towards our bight buoy. The lifting was continued with great caution, when we had the pleasure of seeing the cable at the ship's bow at 12.45 A.M. Steps were immediately taken to get stoppers fixed on the two sides of the bight and to free the grapnel. This was successfully done by 3 A.M., when we began to haul inward. It was found necessary to relieve the strain by cutting away the cable to the west of us. At 3.30 we had got it safely on board, and the end was then taken slowly along to the testing-room in the middle of the ship. It had much the appearance of a funeral, a lot of men carrying the cable along the deck at the slow pace at which we hauled it in. Now came the most anxious quarter of an hour I ever spent in my life. The end was carried into the testing-room and connected to the instruments; all the faces standing round as though each was expecting to hear a judge deliver a sentence of death or acquittal. Now we were to learn whether all our labour had been in vain or not. Were we in perfect electrical connection with Ireland or not? We had got up the cable. We had done so before, but it would not speak to us. For nearly fifteen minutes did we bear the intense excitement while the operators were endeavouring to get the attention of those in charge at Valencia; then it came, that little magic light flashed upon the scale, and one wild burst of pent-up feelings was given by ringing cheers, which were taken up by those outside, and oh, what a load was lifted from my heart! As soon as the tests had satisfied our electricians that all was right the splicing of the two ends together was commenced, and at a few minutes before seven this morning the pleasant hum of the paying-out machinery was heard, and our thread was again streaming away over the stern of the ship. Yes, that low hum of the wheels and the splashing of the break-wheels in the water-tanks in which they run have been to me for a long time this morning the most delicious music I ever heard, and after a night's anxiety and labour soothed and calmed one's feelings. The cable has come up in the most perfect state—in no way different from what it was as laid down. We must now pay it out very slowly and make sure of our work. We will, I trust, reach Heart's Content on Saturday next. The *Medway* and *Albany* are picking up the buoys left down, when the latter will proceed direct to England. She got our letters this morning.

Sunday evening.

All has gone well during the day, the cable having run out steadily at a slow speed. At noon we were in lat. 51° 56', long. 36° 50'.

Monday, September 3rd.

We were fortunate in getting the cable when we did, as if we had not, all our previous efforts would have been thrown away, for since last night it has blown a gale of wind, and continues to do so, although not quite so bad now as it has been during the day; but the seas have been running mountains high, and the poor *Medway* has been having a very unquiet time of it. All has gone on well with the cable, but at twelve last night there was a slight alarm as the coil in the tank caught the following coil and pulled it away; the men had no difficulty in freeing it, but they shouted up to stop the ship, which was done for a few seconds. Fortunately, I knew nothing of it until this morning, and had a good night's sleep until it was time to get up for breakfast at 7.30. I feel glad another day is gone, as each day past lessens our risk, and it would be hard to have any mishap now with the cable. On Wednesday night we will be in comparatively shallow water, and then we need not care. Our position to-day at noon was lat. 51° 34', long. 39° 8', so that we have only run ninety-four miles since yesterday, a poor day's work. The amount of cable paid out was 126.64 miles. We had a lot of news to-day from England. During this afternoon we have had some sail set on the ship to steady her rolling, a little piece of amusement she has been very much inclined to practise.

Tuesday, September 4th.

All has gone well with our cable to-day; we have not made a very long run, and the amount of slack payed out since we started has been very large, amounting to 26.5 per cent. I know not how to account for this, as the strain on the dynamometer has been from 14 to 16 cwts. Probably it will come out right in the end, as it did last time, but at the present rate we will be short of cable. I, however, have no fear on this score; the slack cannot really be much in excess of our usual average.

Wednesday, September 5th.

Thank God another day is gone, although it may seem wrong to wish our time in this life to be shortened even by one day; yet to those who hour by hour look at that small line running out at the stern of this ship and feel, as I do, that each passing hour brings us nearer to safety, it is a cause for relief that we are now within a few hours of the time when we will be in shallow water and no real harm can happen to us. How glad will I be when all this work is complete! It is a long time to go on from hour to hour in a state of anxious suspense. Weeks have accumulated, and still the hours of anxiety have continued.

Thursday, September 6th.

Thank God we are now out of all danger and can with certainty say we can lay the cable. We are now in shallow water, and will land the cable on Saturday afternoon. To-day has been a beautiful day, good enough for grapnelling, but thank goodness we have not got this operation to perform. Both the sea and wind have been very calm, and all has been going on as well as it is possible for it to do.

Friday, September 7th.

We will make Heart's Content early to-morrow morning, and, I hope, get the shore-end laid before very late in the afternoon, and then we will be ready for a start home on Sunday. To-day at noon we were in lat. 49° 8', long. 51° 26', and had run 134.8 miles, so that we did a good day's work. The cable in our main tank will be a very close fit, but I hope it will take us in. We have some fifty or sixty miles more, but shall be glad to avoid making a splice.

HEART'S CONTENT, *Saturday, September 8th.*

I thank God we are permitted once more to dip our anchor in this little harbour, and to say our two years of labour and anxiety are completed. We have now fulfilled the task we undertook, and our second cable is safely landed on the coasts of Newfoundland amid a salute of twenty-one guns from the *Terrible,* the *Lilly,* and the *Great Eastern,* and the cheers of our own people and a few besides assembled here to see the cable landed. I know of nothing in the course of my life in which I have taken so deep an interest—an interest more intense than I will now allow myself to take again in any enterprise. But I feel I am fully rewarded. We have succeeded in doing what ninety-nine out of one hundred people have declared to be impossible. We have now completed two lines of the most perfect and, I feel sure, enduring lines of telegraphic communication between England and the continent of America, and this under no slight difficulties.

And I was more than pleased to see by the papers we got to-day that our efforts have been noticed by the Queen in her Speech on closing Parliament. I do not know if such a thing was ever done before, but in any case we can have no higher praise, and I will ever feel proud of the part I have acted in the matter. When the instruments were connected I sent the following telegram to Lord Stanley:—

September 8*th*.

"Mr. Gooch has the pleasure to inform Lord Stanley that the cable of 1865 was recovered from the bottom of the Atlantic on the second of this month, and has been safely landed to-day at Heart's Content, the recovered cable being in the most perfect condition. He also takes this opportunity of saying how much all here engaged on the undertaking were grateful, on receiving a newspaper to-day, to see the kind reference made to their efforts in Her Majesty's Speech on the closing of Parliament."

When I went on deck a little after six this morning, I found the ship stopped in consequence of a fault which had just shown itself in the cable. We were then within eleven miles of Heart's Content; the morning was very fine and calm, and the water as smooth as a mirror. The fault, on test, was found to be in the tank. As we had some spare cable in the aft tank, we cut it away from the middle one and spliced on the other; this, however, delayed us nearly three hours. We then steamed on to the entrance of the harbour, where the *Medway* was ready with the shore-end; the cable was then cut adrift from the *Great Eastern* and the end got on board the *Medway*, and the splice made to the shore-end; the *Great Eastern* in the meantime steaming into the harbour and dropping her anchor. This was done about eleven o'clock;

the splice was not completed until after one o'clock, when she steamed into the harbour, and by four o'clock the end was safely lodged in the electrical room on shore and our work done.

Heart's Content looked quite homely to me to-day. We sail to-morrow, and I suppose I will then take my last look at it. Well, I will never forget it.

Thursday, September 13*th.*

At noon we were in lat. 50° 48' 30", and long. 34° 41' 30", having run 227 miles. We have had all sail set to do as much good as it will. I think this ship is a grand sight with sail, although it is only a small part of what she would need as a sailing-ship, yet from their size they are no mean spread of canvas. The stars are bright to-night when not hid by clouds. I have had a long walk on deck, our saloon is so hot from the funnels, now we are steaming hard, that it is bad to bear the heat. Well, we are now making wide strides each day towards England; the line on my chart grows fast, and will soon reach land on the right side of the Atlantic—not too soon for my taste. Good-night.

Friday, September 14*th.*

It is just eleven weeks to-day since I came on board this ship, and have only been out of her one night. Our progress to-day has not been quite so much as yesterday, having only run 212 miles; but it looks a long stretch on the chart, and puts us only 729 miles from Cape Clear. We were at noon in lat. 51° 1' 30"; long. 29° 3' 30". The day has been very fine, with a light fair wind, but a heavy swell from the north, causing us to roll a good deal. As I write now, I am obliged to spread my legs out as far as I can to prevent my chair sliding about the cabin. I have not been very well to-day—had a bad pain in my side and have felt below par. My quoit-playing yesterday has made me sore and stiff all over, and during last night I slept very badly with unpleasant dreams, and so much aching in my legs I could not rest, so I have taken it very quietly to-day. The days are getting very short now; we have lights at dinner. To-night is a very pleasant night on deck. The moon has just set below a heavy mass of clouds, and it is cloudy overhead, but very much warmer than we have had it. I suppose we now feel the comfort of the Gulf Stream instead of the northern current in which we have spent so many weeks. I begin to think of packing up now, and have done a little in that way to-day. Good-night.

Saturday, September 15*th.*

We have had a very lively time of it since last night; the old ship has been giving us a taste of her rolling. Not a wink of sleep did I get last night. We have been rolling nearly as bad all day, a most uncomfortable state of existence. It is, however, much better now, and I have better hopes of to-night. There has been very little wind, but a very heavy and long swell from the north. There have been showers of rain through the day. We met one of the Cunard steamers the night before last about twelve o'clock, and a brig was seen early this morning, but I have not seen anything in the wide waste of waters since leaving Heart's Content.

Sunday, September 16*th.*

This is the twelfth, and, I hope, last (for some time) Sunday I have been here. My red line on the chart begins now to get very near the Irish coast; a few days more and I will be back at my old occupations, and the past three months will look like a dream, and I will then often think of the hours I have spent in this cabin, and, I dare say, after a little, begin to long for another trip, but not for so long a time. We have had less rolling since last night, and I got a very good night's rest. Although the sea is still very heavy, it has been very beautiful and grand to-day—a bright sunshine on it, and the whole surface covered with breakers and rainbows. We met a large steamer, supposed to be one of the National Line between Liverpool and New York; she seemed to feel the sea very much. It has been a nice day for us, with a very strong breeze in our favour. The Bishop[3] did service for us to-day, and gave us a sermon with two services.

Monday, September 17*th.*
We met two large steamers to-day, one of Cunard's, the *China,* at breakfast-time, and one of Inman's in the afternoon. This has been one of the finest days we have had, and quite a treat after what we have endured. At 2.30 our eyes were gladdened by the sight of land; we then saw the western coast of Ireland, and it has been a pleasant occupation all the afternoon to watch it gradually open out, looking very like home again. The outline of the mountains on this part of the coast is very beautiful, and to-day there was a soft purple haze over them. Between six and seven o'clock the small steamer from Crookhaven came out to us for telegrams. A case containing some was thrown overboard for her. The people on board of her—and there appeared to be a good many—gave us a good cheer as a welcome back. At eight o'clock we were at the Fastnett light. This was the evening fixed for the theatricals to come off, so we dined at five to enable them to prepare the saloon by nine. What was acted was written by Dean and Poore; they had taken a deal of trouble to get it up, but it went rather heavy, not nearly with the life the last one did. They were so long between the scenes that we got rather tired of sitting with our nose over some smoking oil-lamps at our

feet, with a large flag as a drop-curtain within three or four feet of your face. The Bishop seemed to enjoy it very much; he had not seen any theatricals for forty years. Well, to-morrow night, if all goes well, we will be off Liverpool. The night is cloudy, and does not look like a fine day to-morrow; I hope it may, as we will be a good deal in sight of land, if clear weather. If we do as we hope, we will get into Liverpool by the early tide on Wednesday morning, and enable me to get home for dinner. As it is now very late I will get to bed; to-morrow will be a busy day packing up. How long a time it seems since I was unpacking! Good-night.

Tuesday, September 18th.

Here we are once more on the shores of old England; we have just passed the lights on the Island of Anglesea, and are now making for Liverpool. I suppose in half-an-hour we will take the pilot on board. Thank God our voyage is over, and we come home to say we have done all we started to do.

Mr. Spencer H. Walpole, the Home Secretary, called at my office to see me on the 21st September, but as I was not there, he wrote to ask me to go to his house and spend the afternoon with him on the Sunday following, the 23rd. This I did, and he then told me Lord Derby had asked him to see me and ask me if I would accept a Baronetcy; and in the *London Gazette* of the 13th November 1866 the following appeared:—

"WHITEHALL, *November* 10*th,* 1866.

"The Queen has been pleased to direct Letters Patent to be passed under the Great Seal, granting the dignity of a Baronet of the United Kingdom of Great Britain and Ireland unto Daniel Gooch, of Clewer Park, in the county of Berks, Esq., and the heirs male of his body lawfully begotten."

And I was a Baronet, a fate that had certainly never entered my head. Any acknowledgment of my services by the Government had certainly never formed any part of my hopes. I had gone into this matter of the cable from a desire to assist in completing so great a work, and would have been quite content with feeling I had had success. When all equally did their best, it seemed to me unfair that a few should be selected for any special reward. I earnestly pray that the dignity thus conferred upon me by the Queen may never be disgraced by myself, or those who, in the course of nature, will succeed me.

1. Now Admiral Sir J.E. Commerell, G.C.B.
2. Now the Earl of Derby.
3. Bishop Field of Newfoundland had been given a passage home.

V

THE ATLANTIC CABLE-LAYING EXPEDITION OF 1869

1867.—The early part of this year was a time of great anxiety to me in railway matters.

I had been appointed a Deputy-Lieutenant of Berkshire early in the year (February 23rd), so was able to attend full dress-parties in uniform. It is a dreadful thing for a thin man to go in a court dress. I was also appointed a magistrate for the county of Berks in the summer of 1867, and attended the bench a few times at Windsor.

1868.—The periodical called *Engineering* had a portrait of me in their number for 21st February 1868, and a short account of my life.

May 23rd.

My wife was taken from me after a painful illness. She was buried at Clewer on the 28th of this month. I spent the summer at Clewer and in Ireland.

October 11*th.*

I was appointed Prov. Grand Master for Berks and Bucks yesterday, so that I must give up my office of D.P.G. Master of Wilts, which I regret.

CLEWER, *November* 24*th.*

My election is over, and I have again been returned for Cricklade.

S.S. "GREAT EASTERN," PORTLAND,
Tuesday, 18*th June* 1869.

Once more I am sitting in my cabin here, getting ready for another Atlantic cable expedition. I well remember how often in this cabin, three years ago, I resolved I would not again go on such an expedition, and probably will often feel the same on this trip; but I love this old ship, and cannot pay her a visit without a strong longing to stay with her. I left town on Tuesday morning, accompanied by the Directors of the Great Western Railway, who have very kindly taken advantage of this occasion to give me a dinner, which was held at the Royal Hotel at Weymouth on Wednesday night. Some of the directors and officers of the Bristol and Exeter, the South Devon, and the Cornwall Railway Companies came; nothing could be more gratifying than the kindness and warmth of the expressions used towards me in the speeches. About fifty sat down to dinner. Mr. Wood,[1] our deputy-chairman, was in the chair. Probably to few men could a more agreeable compliment be made. The men who sat round that table were no strangers to me, but men with whom I had been associated for many years. Some of those who have left our direction were present—Mr. Williams of Chester, Mr. Bodenham of Hereford, and Mr. D. Ogilvie of London. They travelled a long distance to show me a kindness, and I may rightly feel happy in the feeling that years of steady perseverance in the line of my duty have thus obtained the respect and esteem of so many old friends. I brought them on board the ship in the afternoon, with which they were very much pleased, and all went off very well. We kept up our party until nearly twelve o'clock. Yesterday the Mayor and Corporation of Weymouth gave us a breakfast in a tent, but first took us in a steamer to see round the harbour and Portland. Unfortunately the morning was very wet, and we could not stay on deck, but by one o'clock, when the breakfast-time arrived, it cleared up and was a nice bright afternoon. All passed off very well, and at six o'clock I bade good-bye to my friends, and came on board the ship, glad to get the quiet and spare time. We are all in excellent trim for our voyage. I never saw the old ship in so complete a state for a start. We have been a little disappointed about our coals; one of the three steamers that had to supply us with 2000 tons put back from bad weather, and only arrived in the middle of last night. We are taking as much out of her as we can, but do not intend to delay our voyage to take it all. I had a telegram yesterday night, saying the shore-end was laid at Brest in the morning, so that I trust we will make the splice at Brest on Sunday and commence our work across the Atlantic. Great credit is due to Halpin, who was first officer of the ship on her two former expeditions, and now has the command. He has the great, and what I call unusual, power of doing things quietly, yet well. The day is very wet, but I hope it may clear up in the afternoon, as we have given permission to the Weymouth people to come on board and see the ship. We have fixed to leave in the morning at eight.

Friday night, June 18*th.*

We had a large party of visitors on board this afternoon, but it was dreadfully wet for them until between three and four o'clock, when it cleared up and has since been very fine. Sir James Anderson and others came on board. I hope all will be here to-night, or they will stand a chance of being left behind. I have been getting a cot rigged up to-day to sleep in. It will be more comfortable than the fixed berth when the ship rolls.

Saturday night, June 19*th.*

We had a lovely morning for our start from Portland, and were punctual to our time, the ship being fairly under weigh at 8.30. All was done in a quiet and ship-shape manner, and we have had a lovely day. The *Scandinavia* started with us and is in company. Our speed has been about 6½ knots, paddles making 6½ and screw 29 revolutions. It is a great treat to see the paddle-engines doing their work again. The ship is drawing 27 feet forward and 34 feet aft, or a mean of 30½ feet. We passed the Start Light a little before five, and are now crossing over, hoping to be on the French coast in the morning early. The weather has changed this evening, as it is now raining a little, and very cloudy.

BREST, *Sunday night, June* 20*th.*

We made a good run across the Channel last night, and were off Ushant this morning at eight o'clock, but our stupid French pilot said the land we made was not Ushant, and we went off to sea again, until he was lost in his own blunder, and, after wondering where we were, an observation showed us that we had passed to the west of Ushant. So we stood in again, and about one o'clock made the same point we had been at early in the morning. This was very vexing, as it has lost us a tide. The ship made between eight and nine knots during the night. We arrived in Brest Roads about 3 A.M., and found the *Hawk* and *Chiltern* waiting for us. The day has been very fine, and the scene was a very pretty one as we came in, some six or seven steamers having come out from Brest to meet us, but we did not have any one on board, as the sea was rather lively for a small boat. I cannot say I was sorry at this, as we had no wish to see the ship covered with a multitude of people. We had church service on board this morning. I like the homely character of these services. They are more impressive than in a church, to me at any rate. The crew were mustered in their Sunday-clothing before church, and are a better looking lot of men than I thought they were from seeing them about on the deck. The coast round here is very rocky, and not a very safe port to enter, I should think; but it is very well lighted. There are large detached rocks scattered about, showing their heads above the water; all very well in clear weather, when you can see them, but rather awkward in a fog or in the dark.

The party from Paris came off in a steamer, but wisely did not attempt to come on board. It would not have been quite safe for landsmen; indeed, even for sailors it is not a very safe job when there is a little sea on, as the boat may so easily get under our side ladders and be swamped, or the people get their heads crushed. I will now go on deck and see how the work is getting on.

Monday morning, June 21st.

Nothing could have been better for us than the weather and everything else last night, and our splice was made without difficulty, and at two this morning the ship's head was turned for the Atlantic, and our voyage began, not to be interrupted again, I hope, until we reach its end. I went to bed about twelve, after seeing that everything necessary was being done to the splice, and got up again when the gun fired about two this morning to signal our departure, and went on deck, where I remained until 4 A.M., then turned in again. There was a glorious sunrise; but a red one, so we may have some rain before the day is over, but it is up to this time a beautiful day, and the sea like a sheet of glass. Our start has been an admirable one in every respect, the heavy portion of our cable is running out beautifully.

Monday night, June 21st.

This is the longest day, and the end of the first day of our work. All has gone on as well as we could wish. There is some little hitch with the people on shore, as we cannot speak to them, although they speak to us. The electricians are a little puzzled with it, and say it is owing to the arrangement of the cable in our tanks, and that when the heavy end is all out it will be all right. It cannot be any fault in the cable itself, as that is perfect. At noon to-day we were in lat. 48° 18', long. 5° 40', and had run 41 miles from Brest, leaving about 2300 miles to St. Pierre of cable to be payed out. We have seen a great many ships to-day. We had some rain this afternoon for an hour; it then cleared up, but will, I think, rain again before morning. The glass keeps high and steady, the sea is perfectly smooth, and, indeed, the weather is all we could wish. I hope we shall get some news from England to-morrow. We have had none to-day, and I am anxious to hear what the Lords have done with the Irish Church Bill. Although this is the end of our first day, it looks a long time to go on paying out the cable; say 5 per cent. is done. I think I shall be glad when it is done, and I am once again in England. God bless all dear ones there.

Tuesday night, June 22nd.

All has gone on to-day as well as we could wish. The weather has been fine but dull, with the exception of four or five hours in the middle of the day, enabling good observations to be taken at noon. The shore end was all paid out about one o'clock this morning, and we have since been paying out the main cable; it is running out beautifully from the large tank. Tonight, about one, we change to the forward tank. Good messages have been exchanged with the shore to-day, and I was glad to learn the House of Lords had read the Irish Church Bill a second time. I hope they will materially alter its clauses.

Wednesday night June 23rd.

We have had a glorious day to-day. Nothing could have been finer than the weather, bright warm sunshine, enabling capital observations to be made, and all has gone well with the cable. We changed from the main to the forward tank this morning at 1.30, and the cable is running out very well from the tank. As it is now carried the whole length of the ship, our line of lamps to-night looks very well, and gives a good imitation of Oxford Street. Since the change of tanks there has been a difficulty again in speaking with the shore. We have got some messages, though very slowly; but as they are improving, I hope by to-morrow all will be right, and we shall be able to get some news.

Thursday night, June 24th.

We had a fault in the cable this morning at 3.30. The ship was stopped very quickly after the signal was given from the testing-room, the paying-out disc only making sixty revolutions. Stoppers were put on, and the cable cut forward and put upon the hauling-in gear. One and a quarter miles were then hauled back before the fault was got on board, at about a quarter before eight. The splice was at once made, and the ship again under weigh at 9.30. The depth of the water was about 2200 fathoms, and it gave a strain in the dynamometer of about four tons; quite enough, as a good many wires were broken in the cable pulled in. We held an inquest on it this afternoon, and found the fault was caused by a small puncture in the core, which must have been done before it was covered. There is no doubt the extra strain it had in paying out extended the injury sufficiently to bring it to light. It is a great satisfaction to find it is not caused by a broken wire in paying out, as we may hope it is not likely we will find such another fault. The hauling-in gear forward pulled the cable back very well, but with more strain on it than if the engine had been applied to the paying-out gear. As though this fault and its anxieties was not sufficient for us, a false alarm was given at twenty minutes to eleven of another fault. The light flew off the scale and did not come back, from the force with which the mirror had moved causing it to stick. It is supposed some one or other must have touched one of the wires by accident, giving dead earth. The ship was stopped, but as the mistake was quickly discovered, we went on again at once. Nothing could have been more favourable for dealing with such an accident as we had this morning than our weather; indeed, the sea has been like glass, and the day hot and lovely. A swallow came on board yesterday, and we saw some sea-birds round the ship. We have had two or three ships pass us to-day. As our electricians do not seem able to speak with the shore, we have not sent or received any messages to-day. They seem a little at sea as to the cause of this.

Saturday, June 26th, 11.30 A.M.

After the fault on Thursday, the cable went out very well, and seemed going right. During yesterday between 10 A.M. and about 7 P.M. the cable was used for passing messages. They came much better, but still very slow. When Willoughby Smith, after dinner or about 7 P.M., went to the test-room, he resumed the current and then saw a decrease in the resistance. He took steps to try and satisfy himself of the cause and the locality, but was quite unable to do so. About 9 P.M. he told me there appeared to be a small fault or some other cause on shore to account for the change in resistance, but he could not say where, or whether it might arise from some change in the wires on shore. We at once went to Canning, and, after fully discussing the matter, determined to cut off the main and after tanks from the current, and see if any better indications could be obtained on the shorter length. This was done, but the defect still showed itself between the ship and shore. It was then settled to cut off the cable remaining in the forward tank about three hundred miles, so as still further to shorten our circuit; this was done without giving any further information. A consultation was then held with the engineers of the French Company at 2 A.M. I asked the French engineers to give me their opinion frankly, as my desire was to do that which would be best for the success of the enterprise, rather than to consider the interests of the Telegraph Company alone. I regretted I did not get from them any decided opinion as to what was best to be done; but they pointed out the consequences to the shares of the French Company if the cable was constructed with the slightest fault in it. None of them could give me the slightest idea of where the fault might be; indeed, Mr. Jenkins said it might be a ship had injured the cable in Brest. There appeared to be only three courses open to us. One, to go on and try to complete the cable; all seemed to agree that the fault was so slight, it might not for very many years interfere with the working of the cable (Varley said an indefinite time), and should the fault develop itself afterwards, it might then be located and repaired. Another, to begin and pick up the cable in the hopes of recovering the fault. The third, to cut and go back to the shallow water, and lift the cable and test it there, and if there found good to the shore, to splice on to it and go on to lay as much cable as might be left in the ship, buoying the end until more cable could be made and sent out from England to complete it. This third plan appeared to be too uncertain; the second also was a very hopeless task, to begin pulling back cable without the slightest idea whether it was twenty or three hundred miles we might have to recover, and the almost certainty, if it became a work of many days, we would break it in 2400 fathoms of water from weather. I therefore decided to go on. In this view I was supported by all our staff, and we at once began to make the splices and started the ship at 5 A.M. this morning. As though we had not had anxiety enough for one night, a very sad fault showed itself at eight. The ship was at once stopped and the cable pulled in. After getting in three-quarters of a mile the fault was retraced. An examination of this fault shows it to be a clean and sharp puncture of a very similar character to the former one, only this had not the appearance of age about it the other had. The yarn over the hole was discoloured, but it was impossible to say whether it was an old fault or not. The splice was made and the ship started at 11 A.M. These faults are quite a new feature in cable-laying. In 1865 our faults could be accounted for by broken wires, as the piece of wire was found in each, but here is simply a clean hole, and, if done wilfully, we know not how many we may have. It is very trying and enough to turn one's head grey. The weather continues all we could wish and the sea quite smooth. A large number of ships passed us yesterday; at one time fourteen were in sight; we spoke to three and reported them. It is just a week this morning since we left Weymouth.

Saturday night, June 26th.

What an up-and-down life is this cable-laying! For the last twenty hours I have believed we could not now lay a perfect cable on account of the small fault reported in it, and on which some £100,000 depends to the Construction Company. At four this afternoon I was agreeably surprised by Willoughby Smith coming to my cabin and telling me the fault had disappeared suddenly, and up to the present time it remains all right. I trust, therefore, it has only been caused by some derangement of the wires on shore, but what anxiety has it cost me! I will, however, not be too sanguine until another day has passed. I may now be glad I decided as I did last night, not to pick up in search of this fault; we might have lost the cable, and would certainly have lost our time and labour. At present the cable is perfect, and, as I am very tired and weary, I hope I will get a long comfortable sleep to-night. I stood in the paddle-box to-night to watch a beautiful sunset, the first we have had in the Atlantic; the sight is very grand.

Sunday night, June 27th.

I am glad to say the electrical condition of our cable is excellent, and we were able to report it perfect to day. God grant it may continue so. We will finish the forward tank to-morrow night. The ship is now more than seven feet by the stern. There is a very heavy dew, making the decks quite wet, but the sun set like a continuance of fine weather. I had a telegram saying all was well in England.

Monday night, June 28th.

The weather to-day has been bright, hot, and lovely—the sea like a lake. A couple of whales were alongside the ship, also a sunfish and a flying-fish. It is unusual to see the latter fish so far north, and must indicate fair weather. We certainly have so far been wonderfully favoured with the weather. Our cable has gone out very well to-day, and we have just changed from the forward to the after tank between ten and half-past; the change was done in a very quiet and admirable manner. Our ship is some eight or ten feet down by the stern, although we have got water in her bows. She will now come up quickly again as the after tank empties. The supposed fault has shown a loss of resistance again this morning. They have been working the cable with 100 cells. This has now been reduced to twenty. It is a very provoking thing this defect, as we do not seem able to place it at all, nor indeed do our people feel certain it is a fault; it is so small, and the same effect may be produced from other causes. How difficult it is to get a line 2600 miles long without so much as the prick of a pin in it, and to get this safely stretched across the ocean! This matter showing itself again has a little disheartened us, and we are not a very cheerful party to-day.

Tuesday, June 29th.

All has gone on well to-day in paying-out the cable. The weather has been very fine, but much cooler, and this evening there is a good deal of wind and rough sea from the south. Some of the sailors say it is going to blow, while others say not,—time will show. We are now a little over half way through the deep water on to the southern point of the banks of Newfoundland; if all goes well, another week will take us there, when we have only 360 miles to lay in shallow water, and then home to England. How glad I shall be to see the ship's head turned in that direction, our work finished! The cable continues to improve in insulation, although the question of a fault or no fault is an open one yet between our electricians and the French ones.

Wednesday morning, June 30th, 11 A.M.
Those who said it was going to blow were certainly right last night; it is now blowing a very heavy gale from the south-east, and we had the additional misfortune to have a fault at five this morning. The light was seen to fly off the scale and immediately return, and in five minutes it again left it not to return. The ship was at once stopped and hauling in begun, but the gale was too much for us, and after getting a strain in the dynamometer of five tons, the cable parted,—fortunately between the paying-out machinery and the hauling-in gear forward. It was also very fortunate that the paying-out machinery and the stoppers held the end. It was at once buoyed, and now rides by the buoy in the middle of the Atlantic. This is a great trouble to us. I cannot understand these constant faults, as we find nothing like broken wires to account for them. It was also very singular that the light left the scale five minutes before the fault was again seen, as though some sharp instrument had been pushed into the cable and at once withdrawn again. One does not like to suspect men of such wickedness, yet it is hard to believe these faults accidental, particularly as we had not a single one during the time the cable was being manufactured and stowed into the tanks. The storm is now raging in a mad way, wind and rain, and a very heavy sea; we are putting down a mark buoy. The *Scandinavia* was

told to do so also, but after trying, we saw she gave up the task. It is awful to see these ships with the seas running clean over them; it makes one dread every moment seeing them go down. I cannot say I am sorry they are out of sight. I have stood on the bridge compass-house for a couple of hours watching them. I at times felt that the bridge-house itself would be blown away. Anderson thinks the gale is too heavy to last long; the glass fell five-tenths of an inch, he says. It is a very heavy gale,—I have certainly not seen anything like it before, although I have seen larger waves. We must hope it will quickly subside, and that we shall be fortunate in recovering our end again; if not, I fear we must grapple for it, and then our work is very uncertain. It has fortunately happened in the shallowest water we have in the mid-Atlantic, being only between 1800 and 1900 fathoms. The fault was very nearly in when the cable broke, but if we had got it in, the gale increased so much we could not have held on to it to splice.

Wednesday night, June 30th.

Both wind and sea have gone down a good deal, but the glass is still falling, and very different opinions are held as to the chances for to-night and to-morrow. We saw our buoys a little before dinner, one on the end of the cable and two mark buoys; they seemed all to be riding very well. We have been performing the very disagreeable duty all day of driving to windward for ten or twelve miles and then turning round and running back again. Some of these turns in the cross seas gave us a very lively roll. There has not been much rain since morning. The old ship has behaved very well, and has as a rule been very steady. We can now do nothing but look after our buoys until we get fine weather.

Thursday, July 1st.

The weather and sea to-day have not been such as to make it safe to attempt getting the cable on board.

Friday, July 2nd.

I remember when a boy being much interested in reading a book called "Lights and Shadows of Scottish Life."[2] If I had the skill, I think one might write an equally chequered description, of the lights and shadows of cable-laying life. We have just started on our voyage again with the cable all right over our stern. The morning was all we could wish for picking up the buoy, and this work was begun between four and five this morning, and the end safely got on board by 7.30, and by eight the fault was in, the splice made, and the ship started at 10.30. We may indeed be very thankful we have got so well out of our difficulty, and we must only hope we have now had our share of them. I have just had a telegram from Osborne in answer to one I sent him a couple of hours ago; he says the French shares fell to 18 on the news of our trouble. The *Scandinavia* and *Chiltern* are picking up our mark buoys. I had a list of the people on board taken out yesterday; there are 443.

The cable was recovered over the stern this morning. All arrangements had been made to do so at the bow, had the weather been at all unfavourable; but this being all we could wish, it was done at the stern. The long lead of the cable along the deck from the machinery forward, and so on through the machinery aft, has this advantage, that there is most strain on the cable between these two points, and if it breaks, as it did on Wednesday, it is most likely to go there, and we have a little chance of securing the end before it gets overboard. I am therefore of opinion that this is the best arrangement, and we ought not to put the steam-engine again at the stern.

The leading sheaves would be better, I think, if they were a good deal larger, which can easily be done.

Friday night, July 2nd.

We examined the fault this afternoon. It, like the others, is a puncture, and the shape of this is exactly the shape of one of the scarfs of the iron wire round the cable. I have no doubt in my own mind it is caused in paying out by one of these scarfs being broken and sticking into the coil below it in the tank. It is very provoking, as there is no kind of security that we will not have a great many more of these. As a precaution, we have put one of the officers of the ship into the tank with each watch; but I have given up all idea of its being the result of malice. This wire would hardly be put in so clean if done by a man's hand—it would be turned a little in the wound. We must, therefore, hope for fine weather, so that, if a fault does show itself, we have a better chance of cutting it out. The weather has been very fine all day, and there is every prospect of its continuance; the sunset was beautiful. There were a number of birds round the ship to-night, and some fish called skip-jacks were seen. It is not usual to see them so far north. They are a small fish and jump out of the water.

Saturday night, July 3rd.

Our cable has gone out all right to-day. We have put one of the officers of the ship and one of the French electrical staff to watch in the tanks. Although I don't think the faults were caused by a wilful act, yet it is wise to take every precaution in our power, and we are now coming to our deepest water—in fact, the deepest water in which a cable has ever been laid, or 2760 fathoms, or a little over three miles. I should be sorry to try the experiment of having to do anything with the bottom of this part. A little after 5 P.M. today the light left the scale again for a minute, and made us all very anxious. It spoiled my dinner, for I could not eat. Just as we finished, Willoughby Smith came down and told me he had been in communication with the shore, and found one of the stupid clerks there had caused it by putting his hand on a naked wire. This carelessness is very vexing, as it gives us great and unnecessary anxiety; but it is very satisfactory to learn the cause in this case, as it no doubt explains the same things which have occurred before, and been the cause of much discussion and anxiety. But I wish we had the careless fellow here, and we would drum him round the ship. We have got sufficient real cause for anxiety without being bothered with stupidity. We had a good deal of news from shore to-day. I was glad to learn the Great Western Bill has passed the Lords. We also heard the Lords had been dealing with the Irish Church Bill in a way Gladstone does not like. We must try some better plan of joining the ends of the iron wires; the present scarf system will not do. We had very heavy rain this morning from about seven until eleven, when the wind got up and cleared it off, and the rest of the day has been very fine. Good sights were obtained at noon. Several ships have been in sight to-day. We spoke to one this evening and have reported her. If all goes on well, another week will put us out of danger. Just a fortnight to-day since we left Portland.

Monday night, July 5th.

All has gone well to-day with our cable, and its insulation is improving very rapidly as we get it into the water. The day has been fine, with a strong head wind, and to-night the wind seems getting up. I hear the sea pretty rough outside my cabin. Some ships passed us very close this afternoon, but very few of the ships we fall in with have flags enabling them to speak to us.

Wednesday, July 7th.

I was unable to write last night, as the ship was rolling so heavily I could not burn a lamp in my cabin, and the candles hung up do not give sufficient light. The gale was very heavy up to yesterday evening, blowing from the N.N.W., and has left such a heavy beam sea, that we are rolling in a most uncomfortable manner. Getting our dinner was a task of no slight difficulty. In saving a tureen of soup I got a jug of milk over me. I felt the comfort of a cot last night, as, while no one else got a wink of sleep, I was very comfortable, and with the help of the doctor's stuff got a good sleep, only disturbed at times by hearing things rolling about and heavy seas breaking with the noise of thunder under the paddle sponsons, making the ship tremble. Some of the rolls were measured at 28 degrees. The gale was a very heavy one, and the *Scandinavia* fell astern almost out of sight early in the morning, but picked us up again in the middle of the day. Both ships were shipping awful seas. They at times disappeared in a mass of foam, and rose up again on the crest of the next wave with the water pouring off their decks like waterfalls. I cannot say I should like to be with them. The wind went down towards evening, and there is very little of it this morning, but it has left a very heavy beam sea, and we are rolling very heavily; it is with difficulty I can keep my seat to write. Fortunately all has gone on well with our cable, although, when the ship rolls and the cable is running out near the eye, it flies about a good deal and requires close watching. The insulation of the cable is improving very much. We join on the main tank this afternoon, and by about ten to-night will finish the after tank. If all goes well for forty-eight hours more, we will be in shallow water, and this will be a great relief to us all. It is a very anxious work on this deep water. Over three miles is an awful depth. There has been very little increased strain on the dynamometer in the deep water. We have had a good lot of shore news the last two days. The Lords appear to be making important changes in the Irish Church Bill. I think I may be back yet before that question is settled. I am glad the Great Western Bill has been read a third time by the Lords, but regret to see so small an increase in our receipts.

Thursday morning, July 8th.

The heavy sea continued all day yesterday and our rolling also. I was unable to work at night. We had a very bad time of it at dinner, for it seemed to select that particular time for making its worst effects. It is rather fun to see the struggle every one has to make to keep his place at the table, and also to look after his plate and glasses. A dreadful amount of breakage takes place. The day yesterday was very fine, a nice bright sun and very pleasant temperature for sitting on deck. We coupled the main tank in the afternoon, and changed from the after to main tank at 9.30 at night. It was very well done. The engines were stopped and reversed in eight seconds, and the ship was stopped dead in less than 100 fathoms, or her own length. The sea has gone down very much during the night, but there is still a good deal of roll. We had heavy rain at seven this morning, but the day is since fine although cloudy, and I fear we will not get an observation at noon. By twilight we will get into 1800 fathoms water, and by daylight in the morning about 800, and during to-morrow turn round the tail of the Bank of Newfoundland, so that I hope we will be past all serious trouble. Our cable is running out of the large tank very well. We have just had a meeting in my cabin—Sir James Anderson, Halpin, Canning, and myself—to determine the point we are to make for on the tail of the Bank, and Anderson has marked on my chart the course we settled. There are strong symptoms of ice ahead of us. Last night the temperature of the water fell from 67 degrees to 52 in a couple of hours. I should like to see some good large icebergs, if they were not in our way, and would not come across our path in the dark.

Friday morning, July 9th.

The heavy swell has continued, so that we still feel the rolling of the ship too much for a lamp to be quite safe on my table, so I did not write any last night. The day continued very fine, and our cable has run out admirably. I am very thankful to say we are now getting into shallow water. By two o'clock we shall be in 700 or 800 fathoms. The *Chiltern* has gone ahead to take soundings in the tail of the Banks, and to take up a position in 500 fathoms water, and we will then steer for her. We are now making a point we call A, and will then alter our course due west until we get to the point B, where we turn up north on the west side of the big bank. I am very thankful to God we have reached thus far in safety, and all danger to the success of our work is over. It has been a long and anxious operation; the cable tests are extremely high, higher than the former Atlantic cables, and I hope, when we get the end landed, it will be found that the supposed fault is a myth. It must, at any rate, be very slight in its character. We have been on the look-out for ice since yesterday; the air became very cold in the afternoon, the thermometer in the sun showing only 57°. This morning it is only 50°, but there is no sun. We have had a little fog in the distance, but only for a short time. The wind is blowing a good breeze from the north, and this is said to be the best possible wind for keeping away the fogs, a very important matter to us for the next few days. We have as yet had no fog,— a rather singular occurrence to pass so long a time in the Atlantic and not have any. A large fish passed very close to the ship yesterday;

I thought he would go under the paddle, he missed by only about six feet, but did not seem to be at all disturbed by its noise so close to him. The sun seems inclined to get out. I hope by twelve they may be able to get an observation, and so fix our position exactly at the tail of the Bank. We ought to be at St. Pierre on Sunday early, and I hope we may be able to leave there for England on Wednesday, and I may then get to Clewer by Sunday fortnight. We have lost three days by the faults.

Friday night, July 9th.

The sun got out quite bright by twelve o'clock to day, and we were able to get capital observations. We exactly made point A on the chart as arranged yesterday, our most southern point, and have since been running due west along the tail of the Bank. At twelve to-night we shall reach point B, and then alter our course north for St. Pierre. We made a good distance up to twelve to-day, and we have now increased our speed a little as we are in shallow water, the cable running out at about seven knots. Our consort ships took two soundings this afternoon, one 840 fathoms, and the other 620. It is quite a pleasure to look at the cable running out of the large tank, and at night, when the tank is lighted, the effect inside is very pretty. Halpin gave us some champagne to-day to celebrate our arrival in shoal water. It is a great relief to every one, and they all show it in their faces and conversation, like people suddenly relieved from a great weight on their mind. We are most fortunate in the weather; we had every reason to expect to be in fogs, and instead we have had the most lovely afternoon we can imagine, and to-night the sunset was most glorious, beautiful far beyond the power of words to express or of painting to delineate. The sea was a sheet of glass, and the sunset behind a heavy fog-bank which seemed

to enclose the view, making it like a lake with a margin of
trees and mountains. It was a scene never to be forgotten.
We cannot hope for such weather to continue. I fear fogs will
come, and I will have the pleasure of hearing the fog-whistle
just over my head. We have been unable to get news the last
few days owing to the rolling of the ship making the light fly
about on the scale, but we have got some this afternoon. I
have never known the rolling continue so long as it has this
time. I think for three days we have had the fiddles on the
tables; to-day we did without them. Beckwith has been to
work getting his paddle floats ready to put on; only half the
number are on at present, this looks like getting toward the
end of our work, and I shall be very glad when we make our
start home. Jenkins telegraphed to-day that the cable may
now be considered successfully laid.

Saturday night, July 10*th.*
I was awoke this morning by the sounding of the steam-
whistle, and when I went on deck I found it pretty thick,
and could have imagined myself at Paddington Station,
with the constant whistling of the three steamers and the
bleating of the sheep. Towards ten o'clock the fog cleared
away, and since then the day has been beautifully fine. The
sunset to-night with a strong indication of wind and rain
before morning. Our cable has gone out very well, and at
a good speed of seven knots, and the ship has made a good
run, but an error in the compass has placed us too much
by about twelve miles to the S.W., and into deep water or
some 1200 fathoms. The compass error was not discovered
until observations were taken this afternoon, so there is no
doubt our course since twelve has still been too much to
the S.W. We are now hauling up stiff to the north, so as to
strike the shallow line again. The consort ships have been

sounding, and will go ahead and sound again to-night. As far as the cable is concerned, it is an advantage to have it in deep water, as it is safer than in the 100-fathom line on the Bank, but not so safe for us who are laying it. We saw a very curious effect of mirage this morning. A large ship on the horizon was upside down, sailing on her mast-head, and her hull up in the clouds; it is a singular effect; beyond her was a heavy fog-bank. It was very easy to imagine land to-day in the distance on many occasions.

Sunday night, July 11th.

I feel deeply grateful to God for His great mercy in permitting us to complete our work. As I look back on the voyage of now three weeks, how many difficulties have we had to encounter, how much of discouragement; yet we have struggled on full of confidence. I never doubted we should lay the cable; my only fear was, we might lose it, and have weeks delay in picking it up, and my only doubt was the question of time, not the ultimate success. We have lost three days on the road, but here we are in fifty fathoms, and to-morrow will be free from the cable. It came on very foggy last night, and rained in torrents, so that it was difficult to steer our course; frequent soundings were made, and so we have fished out our way to what we call point B, the place where the William Cory had to meet us. During the night I was called up to learn that a kink had taken place in the cable as it left the eye of the coil in the tank, but fortunately it untwisted itself as it went over the top of the tank; had it got into the machinery, it might have given us trouble. When I went on deck this morning the fog was very thick, and our whistle has been anything but agreeable since daylight, and has almost driven one mad all the morning. We had no church this morning, as the officers and hands were needed on deck. When we went on deck after lunch, the fog was beginning to clear away, and by two o'clock it lifted up, and, much to our joy and satisfaction, there was the *William Cory*, not a mile ahead of us, and exactly in our course. I was doubly glad of this for Captain Halpin's sake, as the fact proved him to be right to a yard; nay, I doubt if he would not have run the *William Cory* down, so exactly did he hit the point where she was. Indeed, he took up her position. The lifting of the fog at the moment it did was a kind act of Providence. It has been quite clear all the afternoon, and we have followed our pilot ships; but now the fog has come on again, and we can see nothing, and our whistle is hard at work, likely, I fear, to interfere with one's night's rest. The completion of such a work as this makes me feel very joyous.

Monday, July 12*th.*
The fog continued very thick all night, but we followed our pilot ships up to the buoy where the shore end finishes. As we could not see it, we went on a couple of miles beyond the distance, and then cut the cable from our ship and buoyed the end at nine this morning, hoping to get it clear some time during the day, to make the splice and get on to St. Pierre. But in this we have been disappointed, the fog never having cleared up for one instant, and it has been a long and weary day, nothing to do but blow our steam-whistle, and occasionally fire a gun, but we have not once seen any of the other ships, and have not heard of the *Chiltern.* She would most likely make for St. Pierre when she lost us. We are quite helpless in this fog. Halpin tried to catch some fish this afternoon, but it was a failure; they were not to be caught. When we cut the cable, there had been laid, including the shore ends, 2583 miles, and we have

209 miles left in the main tank, and about four miles that we picked up during the faults. The slack has been 11.14 per cent. on the whole distance. The course come by the ship is only four miles longer than the exact distance measured in the Great Circle. This is very creditable to Halpin and his officers.

MIQUELON, *Tuesday night, July* 13*th.*
When I had finished writing last night, I went on deck a little before ten o'clock, and was astonished at the change in the weather. I had come down only a couple of hours before, leaving it enveloped in a dense and very wet fog; when I went back, all was clear, and the moon and stars were shining bright. This gave us great hopes for to-day, and we were not disappointed. I got up at daylight, and found the beginning of a lovely day. We at once made preparations to give up the cable, or rather to find the two buoys. This took us until eight o'clock, and they were a couple of miles apart. The French engineers wanted to pick up one for a distance, so as not to have so much bend in the cable; this I declined to do; so we spliced on to the shore end, and paid out from the *Great Eastern* a couple of miles to the other buoy, so that on the main cable, the first splice was made in the *Scandinavia*, and the *William Cory* was sent to pick up the other buoy, ready to take the end from us when we reached it. On our coming up to her, we found she had got the buoy but no cable; a pin in the shackle had worked out, and so lost the end of the cable. This was a very vexatious thing, as it was necessary to get the grapnels out in two of the ships and try to recover it. This was not done until three o'clock, when the *William Cory* got it. We then buoyed one end, leaving the small ship to complete the work, as Halpin was anxious to get the *Great Eastern* anchored before dark,

and we had thirty-five miles to go. We therefore started about four o'clock, and came on here; it is in some degree sheltered by the mainland of Newfoundland, and the islands of Great and Little Miquelon and St. Pierre. There was a beautiful sunset as we came in, and our anchor was dropped between 8 and 9 P.M.

Wednesday, July 14th.

The other ships finished their work about 10 P.M., and then came on and anchored near us, so that we formed a strong fleet this morning. The *Gulnare* piloted us into the anchorage. The weather this morning was very lovely and the sea like a mirror.

ATLANTIC, *July 15th.*

Thank God, our ship's head is now turned for England and for home. The work and anxiety of this expedition has been much more severe than the former ones, partly from the length of time it has taken, and also from the faults occurring in the cable.

Friday, July 16th.

This has been a lively and very interesting day. The sea is like glass, with a nice light S.W. breeze, just sufficient to fill our sails, and the old ship looks splendid. It is really a beautiful sight to stand on the top of the paddle-box and see her when all her sails are set. She has been doing about ten knots as an average, but the log shows more, as our course has not been quite a straight one. Our distance has probably been much more than the chart measurement. Her paddles have been making 9 to 9½ revolutions and the screw 33 to 34. We were very much interested during the forenoon in passing through a fleet of icebergs. One was very large. Halpin estimated it at 800 to 900 feet long and very nearly as broad, and about 150 feet high. The colours and brightness of the ice in the bright sun were very beautiful. We went within 300 yards of one good-sized one. All were pretty near. The air was very cold in their neighbourhood. I am very glad to have had this opportunity of seeing them, and under the most favourable circumstances, a very bright sun and clear atmosphere and smooth water. They must be very disagreeable things to run into with a steamer. We also saw some immense flocks of sea-birds, so thick that they cast a shadow on the water. They were very close to it fishing. There was a beautiful sunset and every promise of a fine day to-morrow. The moon is now bright and clear.

Saturday, July 17th.

I am a little disappointed in the distance we have run to-day. I had calculated upon 240 miles instead of 220. The wind has been from the south, not much of it, but we have kept our fore and aft sails set, and appeared to be going quickly through the water, the paddle engines making about nine revolutions and the screw thirty-two. The weather was very fine all day and the sea smooth, but to-night it has come on a heavy rain and looks like more wind. The glass is falling. Yesterday the temperature of the water was only 47°, while the air was 60°, showing we are not far from ice, but we have not seen any more; indeed, we have seen nothing all day, and it is a slow and idle life, but a week of it, after the cable troubles, will do me no harm.

Sunday, July 18th.

We have only made 220 miles again to-day. The night was wet and thick, and it continued so up to eleven o'clock to-day, when the sun came out, and we have had a lovely afternoon, with a nice fresh breeze from the south-west, making all our sails draw well. It would be very pleasant to get home on Saturday night and have a quiet Sunday at Clewer before I begin the bother of my work in London. The sea is very smooth, and this gives our paddles a good chance of doing their best. The speed of the engines is the same as yesterday. We had church service this morning as usual.

Thursday, July 22nd.

We have had another beautiful day, with fair but moderate wind and a smooth sea. Our run has not been quite so long, but we make good progress. A ship passed within a few hundred yards of our stern. It has been very enjoyable on deck, and I have spent a great deal of time on our paddle-boxes. Our sailors have been amusing themselves to-night by getting up a rifle corps. One of the men who acted as officer had a red uniform. Where he got it I don't know, and his men were armed with brooms and handspikes, and his band consisted of an accordion, a fife, and bones. It was an amusement to everybody for an hour to see them do their drill and marching, and got through an hour after dinner very well. The moon is very bright to-night; how beautiful the sea is with the light of a full moon upon it. Saturday afternoon, if clear, we shall see land; and there is little doubt I will land early Sunday morning.

Friday, July 23rd.

The weather has been all we could wish to-day, although not quite so much wind, but the air has been charming and very enjoyable on deck. We have been looking out for the coast of Ireland this evening, as we were off it but a distance of about thirty-five miles, and we did not see it. To-morrow we will see the English coast once more. I need not say how glad we will all be, yet I don't know why we should. This week has been a most enjoyable one; we could not have had better weather if it had been left to our own making.

Saturday night, July 24th.

This is my last night in the ship, for this voyage at any rate, and I leave her with a good deal of regret mixed with pleasure in the thought of getting home, where I will arrive to-morrow evening. We made the Scilly Islands at twelve to-day, the Lizard at 5.30, and the Eddystone a little after nine, so that we will be at Weymouth by five. The day has been a very lovely one, perfectly calm, and our sails have therefore been of no use to us, and our run has fallen off a little in consequence. There is no doubt the sails help this ship a good deal when there is a moderate breeze.

CLEWER, *August 15th.*

We reached Weymouth on Sunday morning, the 25th July, at seven in the morning, and I at once proposed to land. This we did a little after eight, the crew giving us some hearty cheers as we left the ship. It was a lovely morning, and I left her side with feelings of regret.

When I look back upon the results of the last cable expedition, I feel the experience we have gained much strengthens the opinion I had formed from former voyages. That for long, deep-sea work your chance of success is very greatly enhanced by the use of such a ship as the *Great Eastern*. It is very doubtful whether with a smaller ship we would not on this occasion have lost the end of the cable, and I do not think there would be much chance of recovering it at two to three miles depth with a small ship. It may be said, if a small ship was used and a difficulty occurred in bad weather, the cable could be buoyed, as we, in fact, had to do; but out of the three times we buoyed the cable, we only had it done once as it should be—that, fortunately, in deep water. Once we lost it, and another time it was very nearly lost; probably in rough water it would have been lost, so little hold had the stoppers upon it. It is also quite clear to me that the expedition as a whole should be under the command of the captain of the ship. He ought to be qualified by experience for the task. Halpin would be able to do all that could be done to lay a cable. All he would need would be a staff of cable-hands, as he needs a staff of engineers for his engines; but they should be under his command, and not have a divided command, as we have always had. There is much discussion just now as to laying light, and therefore cheap, cables. I do not think they could be laid across the Atlantic. You need a cable of considerable strength, as difficulties are sure to occur. A light cable would be, in my opinion, sure to break; and I doubt whether in great depths it could be picked up, as it would be impossible to tell when the grapnel had hold of it. If the experiment is tried, I will certainly take no share in the work.

WEYMOUTH, "GREAT EASTERN" S.S., *October* 30*th.*
The old ship is here again, taking in coal for her voyage to India with the cable between Bombay and Suez. Captain Halpin is going in command of her. Osborne and I are down here for a couple of days to see all is getting ready. It is pleasant to be on board the old ship again, and I hope she will have a good voyage.

CLEWER, *Saturday, November 6th.*
The *Great Eastern* sailed to-day from Weymouth at 3.40 on her Indian voyage. She has been detained since Thursday by a gale of wind.

1. Afterwards Sir Alexander Wood.
2. By Professor Wilson (Christopher North).

VI

LATER YEARS
1870–1889

January 1st, 1870.

Another year has passed; what are the records to be left behind? As regards myself and children, I have much reason to be thankful, in so far as health and worldly considerations are concerned. The past pages will show my time has to some extent been engaged in a large enterprise, in laying the line of cable between France and America. This is the third cable I have stretched across the Atlantic, probably more than the traffic justifies, and it will take some time to fill them with work. On the Great Western all has gone well, a quiet but sure improvement, and I look forward with confidence to the gradual growth of our dividends, and the general improvement of the financial condition of the Company. And now another year has begun, who will live to see its end?

Thursday, February 17th.

We had a most important meeting to-day of the shareholders of the Great Western Railway, for the purpose of consolidating the stocks or shares of the various sections forming the

Company. It went off very well, and was unanimously approved. I have been for some weeks very anxious about it, and it is a great relief to my mind now it is settled. We intend to do the same with the preference stocks at the general meeting on the 11th of March.

The *Great Eastern* is now laying the British Indian telegraph. She reached Bombay on the 28th January, and started to lay the cable on the 1st February.[1] I hope all will go well with her. It is the first cable she has laid without my being on board.

March 11th.

At the general meeting of the Great Western shareholders to-day, they agreed to the scheme for consolidation of the preference stocks, and I trust we have now put the financial position of the line upon a sound and satisfactory basis. There is no doubt it is a most important thing for the future of the Company, and I am glad it has fallen to my lot to carry through so important a matter.

REGENT'S HOTEL, LEAMINGTON,
Sunday, September 18th.

I was married yesterday at Christ Church, Lancaster Gate, London, to Miss Emily Burder.

NEWCASTLE, *Sunday, October* 23rd.

We had a carriage this morning, and started at 8.30 for Bedlington to spend the day with my old playfellow George Marshall. The morning was wet early, but it cleared up as we started, and we had a very fine day. How familiar the road seemed to me, particularly as we got towards Bedlington. I found my friend very well, and a hearty welcome. We went to church, where there is little change—a new tower has been built—and afterwards walked down the village and half-way to the ironworks. The village is very much changed for the worse, I think, since I was a boy; but perhaps this is not really so, as better houses have certainly been built, but many of my old landmarks are gone. The house in which I went to school as a child of four years old is exactly as it was, with the same pear-trees in front and the green rails. I was told one of the ladies is also still living in it, Miss Robson. I was very glad to pay another visit to the scenes of my boyhood. We returned to Newcastle at night.

March 5th, 1871.

On Friday last we held our Great Western half yearly meeting and paid 3¾ per cent. It is the highest dividend that has been paid for eighteen years, and will, I trust, be the lowest ever paid in the future. The meeting went off very well, with many very complimentary remarks with regard to myself. We agreed to issue a million of 5 per cent. preferred stock, and to alter the gauge on the line from Swindon down through South Wales. It is a large expense, but I feel the time has come when it must be done. My Telegraph Construction meeting was last Tuesday; it went off very well, and we paid a large dividend.

January 1st, 1872.

The Great Western Railway has prospered to a great extent. Our receipts have been very good, and the shares are now at 118. A large rise since I first took the chair, when they were at less than 90. Telegraphs have also done well, and have largely increased in value. Upon the whole the last year has been one of great prosperity.

April 7th.

The half-yearly meeting of the Great Western was held on the 29th February, and we were able to pay a good dividend of 5⅜ per cent. It is long since the Great Western divided such an amount as this, and I hope we may now go on slowly improving. The shareholders passed a resolution, giving me 5000 guineas, in very complimentary terms.

At the next meeting of the Board, held at Paddington on the 21st of March, the following minutes were entered on the minute book:—

March 21st, 1872.

"Referring to the resolution voting a testimonial to the Chairman, which was passed spontaneously by the shareholders at the half-yearly meeting on the 29th ult., it was proposed by Mr. Miles and seconded by Mr. Ponsonby,[2] and resolved unanimously, that the following minute be communicated to the Chairman:—

"That we, your brother directors, avail ourselves of the earliest opportunity to assure you how highly we estimate your services to the Company, both before and since your occupation of the chair, and we congratulate you on their recognition by this act of the shareholders. We feel assured that, although the words of the resolution require no action on the part of your colleagues, you will allow us to express our warm sympathy with those feelings of regard and confidence which are so deservedly entertained towards you by the shareholders of the Company, and which cannot fail to be most gratifying to you and your family."

November 24th, 1872.

The *Daily Telegraph* of Christmas morning presented a very wonderful list of telegrams from all parts of the world sent on Christmas-Eve. It is a mighty thing that has been done in a few years, and it has worked a wonderful revolution.

January 1st, 1873.

I have again entered upon a new year, and in looking over the past, how much reason have we to be thankful to God for His many blessings. In all respects the year has been a prosperous one to me. I have been blessed with good health, and can look back with pleasure upon the expressions of regard and confidence given me by the Great Western shareholders and directors. The only real anxiety in my mind is the state of the working classes. I fear hard and difficult times must come before the present excitement as to wages and time is put upon such a level as will enable the trade of the country to bear it. Coals are nearly double the price they were eighteen months ago, and the men are earning so much in wages that they will only work three or four days a week, and then only part work. So it is to a less extent with most of the trades. If continued, the only result will be to drive the trade from this country abroad, where wages are less. May God avert so sad an evil to this country, and the present year witness a change for the better in the relations of master and workman. The year has opened with a glorious morning, an agreeable change after the constant rain and cloud.

My Old Cabin, "Great Eastern,"
The Nore, *May 13th, 1873.*

Once more I am in my dear old cabin, where I have spent so many hours of anxiety, and many of joy and contentment. It seems as though I had hardly left the ship, everything is so familiar. I left London middle of day yesterday. We reached the ship soon after four. Osborne also came down by the same train. The day was a very lovely one, and the evening has also been very charming,—full moon and beautifully clear. We were only a small party on board. Halpin is captain, and looks as jolly as ever. After dining at seven we had a long stroll on the deck, and went early to bed. I read for half-an-hour, and then went to sleep, although my pillow is a very hard one. This morning all were astir early in the ship, getting up our anchor and casting off the moorings, and by 10 A.M. all was ready to make a start. The tide turned about eleven, and the last anchor having been lifted, we moved slowly and grandly away from our anchorage for the Nore. The day has been all we could wish, and everything has gone on, and we came to anchor here about 1.30, to wait for one of the moorings, and hope to start in the morning about ten for Weymouth. I feel little anxiety about laying this cable, the third between Valentia and Heart's Content; but a much more difficult and anxious task awaits the ship on her way home, viz., to repair the 1865 cable, which broke a couple of months ago about seven hundred miles from Ireland in two thousand fathoms of water. What has caused it to break is a mystery to us. Is it from being stretched over a chasm and gradually weighted with shellfish or weeds, or has it become rotten and so broken from weakness? In the latter case, I fear we will not succeed in picking it up; but every effort will be made, and I feel confident, if it can be done, Halpin will not fail. The present cable is coated with compound, and will be less liable to decay; but, until we know the cause of the 1865 failing, we are quite in the dark as to the fate of these deep-sea cables.

"GREAT EASTERN." OFF THE ISLE OF WIGHT,
May 15th, 1873, 8 A.M.

We picked up our anchor and left the Nore yesterday morning at 10 A.M. Weather fine, although cloudy and rather cold. The old ship steamed along very steadily at about eight knots. We passed Dover at six in the evening, Dungeness Light at eight, and Hastings about 10.30. There were a great many fishing-boats about as well as ships, and we had to shift about a good deal to avoid them, —one large steamer went close across our bows. This morning is fine but cloudy, and we expect to get comfortably in Portland by one or two o'clock. I am not sure I would like to go a voyage again

Friday, May 16th.

We dropped our anchor yesterday about three o'clock after a beautiful voyage down Channel. The day was lovely, and I enjoyed it very much. We did a little over eight knots speed, and got into a quiet berth. The ironclad *Devastation* left Portland for Milford Haven soon after we came in. She is certainly a very ugly looking craft, and one I should not like to sail in. The after part of the hull is only about six feet out of the water, and with the light sea there was on yesterday the waves were constantly washing over her.

FULTHORPE, *Sunday.*

I came home from the ship yesterday, leaving all on board in a very forward state. We never had an expedition in which all our arrangements were in so forward a state; in fact, all is quite complete, with the exception of coaling. This is to begin on Monday, and, as six thousand tons have to be taken in, it will not be completed before the end of the month.

WEYMOUTH, *June 7th,* 1873.

I came down here yesterday; my wife and Charlie[3] came with me; the latter is going the voyage with the *Great Eastern*. I did not go on board the ship yesterday. We took a long ramble and went on board the first thing this morning, and have spent the day on board, returning to the hotel for dinner. Captain Osborne and Barber dined with us. It has been a lovely day, the sea as calm as a mill-pond. Everything on board the ship is in admirable order, and we never started an expedition so complete, not a single thing left to do. Coaling all finished some days ago, and the ship got clean. We had a good lunch on board.

Sunday, June 8th.

We went on board the ship this morning at 9 A.M., and found her all ready with steam up for a start. The day has been lovely, without a ripple on the water. At a quarter past ten the anchor was lifted, and we moved away from the anchorage beautifully, accompanied by the *Hibernian* and *Britannia.* The National Liner had sailed with the Irish shore end on Thursday. We went with the ship until she turned round west, beyond the Shambles Lightship, about seven miles, and then got into the small steam tender, and watched for some time the fleet pass away to the west. It was a grand sight, and I trust under God's blessing the commencement of a prosperous voyage. The *Great Eas*tern was deep, drawing 37 feet 4 inches aft and 31 feet forward, mean 34 feet 2 inches. She had 8296 tons of coals, and with cables, tanks, and water, a total load of 16,405 tons. I felt it very hard to see her steam away leaving me behind, the first time she has done so in crossing the Atlantic for cable purposes, and I should much like to be with her in her attempt to repair the 1865 cable; but this cannot be, and I must remain content. We returned to Weymouth in time for lunch.

July 18th.

The 1873 Atlantic cable was safely landed, without a single hitch as far as the *Great Eastern* was concerned, on the 27th.

The accompanying ships were driven from their course and left behind by a gale. It now only remains to pick up the 1865 cable, and the old ship will have done a good year's work. I confess I do not feel very sanguine as to this; all will depend upon the condition of the cable.[4] We went to a large garden-party at Chiswick given by the Prince of Wales to the Shah of Persia. The day was fine, and the scene a very pretty one. The Queen and all the Royal Family were there.

August 28th, 1873.

The meeting of the Great Western shareholders was held to-day. We were able to pay 5¾ per cent. dividend, a satisfactory result, being ¼ per cent. beyond the corresponding half year, and as all the other large companies had only paid either no increase or a diminution, the meeting went off very well.

January 1st, 1874.

The New Year has opened with a bright and glorious sunny day. May it be the emblem of the peace and happiness of England and of myself and family. I have much cause for thankfulness to God for all the blessings of the past year.

July 1st.

We have just completed the laying of the cable to Brazil. It is a long distance, and has been very successfully done, with the exception of the piece between Lisbon and Madeira. This was laid last year and broken. The ends have been recovered in 2500 fathoms of water and made good. Halpin laid the portion between Madeira and Brazil. It was carried in three ships, so that two splices had to be made at sea. Halpin tells me he does not approve of the great risk of this operation, but thinks that, even at an extra cost, one large ship like the *Great Eastern* is wiser.

My Old Cabin on Board the "Great Eastern,"
Sheerness, *Friday, July* 31st.

I left London to-day at 4.15 P.M. to join the *Great Eastern* at Sheerness, reaching her a little after six. I find the old ship looking very clean and nice, and it seems very natural for me to be sitting in this cabin where I have spent so many anxious and pleasant hours. The anxiety and excitement of starting on an Atlantic cable expedition is very different from what it was in 1865; all now is simply a matter of quiet business, and there is no fuss and no reporters. Captain Halpin is in charge of the expedition. I half wish I was going across the Atlantic with the ship, but am not quite sure this feeling will last until I get to Portland.

Saturday, August 1st.

We got our anchor up to-day at 1 P.M., and at once steamed out of the harbour. The early part of the day was very dull and looked like rain, but the afternoon cleared up, and it has been very calm and pleasant. Our speed is about six knots, drawing 32 feet forward and 31 feet aft. We have just passed Dover, 10 P.M., but at some distance from the shore.

August 3rd.

I left the ship this morning, and return to Clewer by the 12.30 train, reaching home about six.

Sunday, August 9th, 1874.

The ship sailed from Portland to-day direct for Trinity Bay, Newfoundland, as she is to lay the cable this time on her return. A successful and prosperous voyage to her is my sincere wish.

CLEWER, *October.*

During June in this year we narrowed a large part of the broad gauge all south of our main line between London and Bristol. It was done very well by the staff. Thus is the poor broad gauge gradually dying out. It now only exists on our main line between London and Bristol and the Windsor and Henley branches, and as we are mixing the whole of the broad gauge left, by the end of this year we will have narrow gauge over the whole of the Great Western system.

MY OLD CABIN IN THE "GREAT EASTERN,"
SHEERNESS, *Friday night, July 23rd, 1875.*

I came from London to-day to the ship. We sail to-morrow for Milford Haven, where we intend to lay her up, the charter with the Telegraph Construction Company ending this month. It feels very natural to sit in this cabin again, where I have spent so many pleasant and so many anxious hours; and it may be a long time before I have a sail in the old ship again, as I do not know how we are to employ her in the future. But we will not give up hope that some useful work may be found for her, as she is a noble ship and has done good service in the past.

Saturday, 24th.

We got up our anchor to-day at twelve, drawing 19.9 feet forward and 20.5 feet aft. As usual, the old ship could not move without some excitement, and we had several excursion steamers round us as we went away from Sheerness with bands of music and the usual cheering; also great crowds of people on the shore to see us leave the harbour, which we accomplished all well, but very slow, from the dirty state of the bottom of the ship. The morning was stormy, with showers of rain, but the afternoon was lovely. We passed the North Foreland at 6 P.M.

Sunday, 25th.

We were off Brighton this morning at 9 A.M., off Sandown at 3.30 P.M., St Catherine's Head at 5, and Portland Bill at 11 P.M. The day has been a lovely one, with a fine breeze. Paddles doing about six revolutions, and screw twenty-four revolutions. We had a fine view of the coast all the way.

Monday, 26th.

We passed the Start Lighthouse at 8 A.M., Plymouth at 10, Lizard at 5.30 P.M., Land's End at 7.30. It has been a bright and lovely day, and I have enjoyed it very much. When we were off the Lizard there were seven steamers near us, and we had to thread our way with difficulty through hundreds of fishing-boats which did not care to get out of our way. When off the Land's End we had a most glorious sunset, such as can only be seen at sea.

NEYLAND, *Tuesday, July 27th,* 1875.

We were off the entrance to Milford at nine this morning. There was a great deal of fog early, and we had to wait to go in, so that we would have the ebb-tide to anchor. It was past twelve before we made a start for the harbour. We were joined there by some of the *Great Eastern* directors, who went into the haven with us, and we dropped our anchor at 2 P.M. opposite the town of Milford.

December.

On Friday last, the 17th, the Great Western Railway Company took a very important step in taking over the Bristol and Exeter and South Devon Railways.[5]

June 18th, 1877.

Our railway sustained a great loss on the 5th by the death of our locomotive engineer, Mr. Armstrong. His death was very sudden, he having been only a couple of weeks ill. He has been a very valuable servant to the Company, being an able and upright man. I will also feel his loss very much. His department was a very large and important one. Mr. Armstrong was buried at Swindon Church on Saturday the 9th, in the presence of an immense number of sorrowing people. I and some of the directors went to the funeral, and all the officers of the Company were there. No man could be more sincerely esteemed.

LONDON, *November 29th.*

We went to Swindon yesterday to distribute the annual prizes to the young people at the Institution. This institution is working much good at Swindon, and is steadily increasing in numbers. We missed our old friend Armstrong. How year by year vacancies occur in our Great Western ranks! How few of those who began with me are left! One by one they drop off; and the time cannot be far distant when the whole of the old officers will have passed away.

LONDON, *December 28th.*

The directors of the Great Western Railway presented me this year with a portrait of Mr. Brunel, painted by J.C. Horsley, R.A., from the original picture he painted during Mr. Brunel's life. Horsley is brother-in-law to Mr. Brunel. I value the picture very much both for the sake of Mr. Brunel and the kindly feeling of our Board.

October 17*th*, 1878.

I went to-day to the opening of the Severn Railway Bridge. There was a large gathering, and of course a feast. The day was cold and very uncomfortable. Yesterday at the Severn Tunnel we struck a strong feeder of water on the heading under the land on the Welsh side, which is more than our pumps can manage, and we are drowned out until we get more power. This is very unfortunate, as in a few weeks our heading across the Severn would be complete, and I have been looking forward to walking across next month.

March 25*th*, 1880.

Yesterday Parliament was dissolved, and I am not now a member of Parliament. It is nearly fifteen years since I was first elected. I have agreed to stand again, much against my inclination, as I do not feel equal to the worry of an election or the night-work of the House. I had a meeting on the 15th at Swindon with the principal Conservatives of the borough; and as it appeared clear that, if I did not stand, we should lose both seats, little choice was left to me, and they promised to take the work off my hands and relieve me from any canvas or attendance at public meetings.

May 29*th*.

I did not attend any public meeting nor make any canvas. I met a few of my old friends in the evening of the 1st April, and the polling took place on the 2nd, with the following result:—Maskelyne, 4,350; Gooch, 2,440; Neeld, 1,748.

November 19*th*.

I had a meeting to-day of the *Great Eastern* ship directors, and resigned my position of director and chairman. I did so with great regret and reluctance. I have always taken a deep and warm interest in the noble ship, but I do not feel equal to so many cares as I have lately had upon me, and feel compelled to give up some of them. I have been chairman of the ship since the formation of the present company in 1864, and have spent many happy hours on board of her and many very anxious ones. She has done good work; I doubt but for her if we would as yet have the long lines of deep-sea cables. Mr. Henry Brassey took my place at the Board.

January 27th, 1881.

I was appointed Chairman of the Railway Association on the 13th; Mr. Moon, Chairman of the London and North-Western, was appointed Deputy Chairman, which office I had held for the last three years.

We lighted Paddington Station with the Brush electric light at Christmas. It is a good light, but we have not yet got it into certain working. I have no doubt all the difficulties will be overcome.

February 14th.

We have had to excavate 111 miles of snow on the line, varying from three and four feet to ten feet deep at 142 places. The weather has continued very bad.

Saturday, May 26th, 1882.

I have just heard of the death of my old and dear friend, Captain Bulkeley. He is the oldest of our Great Western directors, and his death will be much regretted by us all.

February 8th, 1883.

We had a meeting of the Telegraph Construction Company on the 6th to approve a Bill we have in Parliament to enable us to extend our operations to electric lighting.

To-day we held our Great Western half-yearly meeting, paying 7¼ per cent. dividend. The meeting went off very well, and was held for the first time in our new room, which seemed to answer very well for sound. The shareholders were good enough, on the motion of Mr. Adams, to pass a resolution asking the directors to have a bust of myself executed, at the cost of the Company, to be placed in the new room. It is pleasant to feel that all my anxiety and work for the Company are appreciated by the shareholders.

October 10*th.*

The large spring, that broke out in the Severn Tunnel a couple of years ago, broke out in a fresh place to-day, and much greater in quantity, flooding the tunnel; and a couple of days afterwards the tide rose in the Severn, covering the land and getting down one of our shafts. Fortunately in the first case no life was lost, but in the latter one man was drowned. So high a tide has not been known for a hundred years.

May 4th, 1884.

Since my return home, I have been appointed by the Government on a Committee to inquire into the conditions under which contracts are invited for the building or repairing of ships, including their engines, for Her Majesty's Navy, and into the mode in which repairs and refits of ships are effected in Her Majesty's dockyards.

July 25th.

We went to-day through the Severn Tunnel as far as we could. Works all going on well. The big spring not so heavy as it has been; I hope we are now fully master of it. We returned home at night.

We have finished our Admiralty Committee and made our report.

October 27th.

I went this morning to the Severn Tunnel. Lord Bessborough met me there before lunch, and we inspected the surface work, and after lunch went below. It fortunately happened that the headings were just meeting, and by the time we had finished lunch the men had got a small hole through, making the tunnel open throughout. I was the first to creep through, and Lord Bessborough followed me. It was a very difficult piece of navigation, but by a little pulling in front and pushing behind we managed it, and the men gave us some hearty cheers. I am glad I was the first to go through, as I have taken great interest in this great work, which is now getting fast towards completion. The spring is now about 7000 gallons per minute, but is fully under the control of the pump; and a fresh pump is just ready to start, which will give us very ample power, more than double our present wants. A heading is being driven parallel with the tunnel, so as to turn this water from the line of tunnel, and so enable us to complete this short length of about two hundred yards. The side heading will then be built out. I hope by June or July next the tunnel will be finished.

May 18th, 1885.

Death has been busy amongst my friends the last few weeks. Mr. Samuda died suddenly. Sir Watkin Williams Wynn died a week ago (May 9th), and was buried yesterday. He is an old Great Western director, holding his seat by Act of Parliament. Sir Watkin was a kind and worthy man, very much liked by us all. When I joined the Board in 1865 he resigned and appointed me in his place, as a vacancy could not be made until the meeting in 1867, when I was elected by the shareholders and Sir Watkin resumed his position.

My old friend and brother officer on the Great Western since I joined the Company, Mr. William George Owen, died on the 14th of this month. He has for some years past been the chief engineer to the Company. His serious illness began in August last, and he has gradually got worse since that time. He resigned his position on the railway a couple of months ago. He was a good and trustworthy officer, and much esteemed by all connected with the Company. Year after year fewer of my old friends are left.

June 9th.

Some election meetings at Cricklade have been held. I had an application from the Conservative party urging me to stand again, but I declined.

August 14th.

Parliament was prorogued to-day. I paid it my last visit on Tuesday the 11th, not sorry to feel my work as a member of Parliament is at an end.

Saturday, September 5th.

I took a special train to-day through the Severn Tunnel. We had a large party, and all went off well. This tunnel is a big work, and has been a source of great anxiety to me. The large spring of water we cut on the Welsh side, a short distance from the Severn, has been a great cost and trouble. I hope, now the arch is finished, it will keep out any serious quantity of water. It will be some months yet before we can open to the public, as the permanent pumping and ventilating machinery has to be arranged and fixed.

The Great Western held their one hundredth half-yearly meeting on the 13th August, and I have attended ninety-four, or, I think, ninety-five of them—a long service. All passed off well.

Wednesday, November 18th, 1885.

The Queen dissolved Parliament to-day, so I am no longer a member of Parliament, after over twenty years' service. It is a great relief to me to feel I am not to be mixed up in the coming contest. The House of Commons has been a pleasant club. I have taken no part in any of the debates, and have been a silent member. It would be a great advantage to business if there were a greater number who followed my example. I have no doubt I will sometimes miss the attendance at the House.

Saturday, January 9th, 1886.

A coal-train was worked through the Severn Tunnel to-day from Newport and Cardiff to Bristol and on to Southampton.[6] All went well, and I hope to open for goods and coal on the 1st March. This has been a very anxious work for me, we have had so many difficulties. One has felt a doubt whether we ought to persevere with so large an expenditure, but I never lost hope of succeeding in the end. Curiously enough, our trouble has not been under the Severn but on the Welsh side under land, where the water has been our difficulty, and now we must pump a great deal more than I had hoped. We had a pressure of 60 lbs. on the inch on the brickwork, and this found its way through. We are now putting pumping-power to the same, with a daily discharge of 30,000,000 gallons. The autumn and winter have been very wet, so I hope in dry weather this will be greatly reduced.

January 20th.

The Mersey Tunnel was opened to-day by the Prince of Wales. It is a big work, and may, in time be of use to the Great Western if there is a good central station built in Liverpool.

September.

We opened our Severn Tunnel on the 1st for goods traffic. The first train that passed through was a goods leaving Bristol at 6.35 P.M. Fourteen trains were worked through during the night, and all was most satisfactory. This has been a long and very anxious and costly job. Our estimate for it was about £900,000. We have now spent over £1,600,000. The water is still a large expense to us, but it is under perfect control. I spent yesterday with Sir John Hawkshaw at Sudbrook, where our chief pumping machinery is.

December 1st, 1886.

We opened the tunnel to-day for passenger traffic. It has been a long and very anxious work for me. But I trust it will prove a very beneficial work for the Company.

January 23rd, 1887.

The *Times* this morning contains the sad news of the death of my oldest friend, Sir Joseph Whitworth. We have lost the first mechanic of the age. I first knew Whitworth in 1836, when I was about to join the Hawkes in the proposed engine-works at Gateshead, and I went to Manchester to order tools; since then we have been fast friends.

August 14th.

This is my Great Western Railway jubilee-day, it being fifty years to-day since I entered the service of that Company, a few days before I was twenty-one years of age. I was very young to be entrusted with the management of the locomotive department of so large a railway; but I felt no fear, and the result has been a success. I have seen great changes during the fifty years. How few of those who entered life with me, or were connected with the railway world at that time, are left to us! Yet we have a very few. God has greatly blessed me in every way.

Sunday, October 16th.

I have sustained a great and grievous loss in the death of my friend Mr. Grierson.[7] He went to Milan to attend a railway conference held there, and returned home on the 29th September, not feeling very well; but he went to Paddington from Marlow (where his family have been spending the summer) on Friday, returning to Marlow that night. On Saturday he was very ill, and continued so until his death on Friday evening, the 7th October, at 7.30 P.M. He was buried at Barnes Cemetery on Wednesday the 12th October. His loss to me and the railway interest cannot be replaced.

May 19th, 1888.

Our Great Western superintendent of the line, Mr. G.N. Tyrrell, retired on Saturday last. He has been forty-six years in the service, and was a most excellent officer and a kind and worthy man. I will miss him very much.

CLEWER, *July 16th.*

We had a jubilee dinner, on Wednesday the 11th, of the opening of the first portion of the Great Western Railway from London to Maidenhead on the 4th June 1838. It was attended by most of the directors and the chief officers. We also had the pleasure of having Mr. Walpole, an old Chairman of the Company, with us. The dinner was at the

Great Western Hotel, and all went off very well—a party of thirty-one.

Dean gave me a very fine photograph of the old locomotive, the *North Star*.[8] She was one of those that opened the line, and we have kept her in a building built for the purpose at Swindon, as a specimen of the engine of the period. I feel a great interest in this old engine, and am glad to have so good a photograph of her. There is also a good photo of the *Lord of the Isles*, an eight-wheel engine which was in the 1851 Exhibition. This was one of a new and powerful class of engine I built about that period. Several of them are still doing our express broad-gauge work, and are equal in every respect to any we have since built. The *Lord of the Isles* is also put away at Swindon to be preserved as a specimen of this class of engine.

August 26th, 1888.

A paragraph in the *Standard* looks like the last of the grand old ship, the *Great Eastern*. I would much rather the old ship was broken up than turned to any base uses. I have spent many pleasant and many anxious hours in her, and she is now the finest ship afloat. Some good use might have been made of her.

November.

The *Great Eastern* has been sold in detail. Poor old ship, you deserved a better fate.

December 11th.

The oldest officer of the Great Western Railway Company died on Sunday the 9th, Mr. T. Merriman Ward. He entered the service in September 1833, before the Act was passed, and held the position of Registrar until February 1st, 1876, when he retired on a pension. He was a good servant and a very worthy man.

February 17*th*, 1889.

I have been very little out of the house since the 17th of last month, when I went into the city and took fresh cold, getting an attack of bronchitis. On the 5th I got down to the station to settle our Great Western Railway report and accounts, and again on the 14th to hold our half-yearly meeting. I got through it pretty well, and as we paid 7¼ per cent. it went off very well.

HASTINGS, *April* 14*th*.

We came down here yesterday by the 3.40 P.M. South-Eastern train. On the 4th March I was attacked with gout in my left foot, and a week after in my right foot, and I have been laid up ever since. I can now walk a little—but very little—and am sent down here to effect a cure.

Saturday, April 27*th*.

We left Hastings to-day by the 2.30 P.M. train. The South-Eastern gave us a saloon carriage, so we made our journey very comfortably. I do not find my visit to Hastings has done me much good. I hope I will feel the benefit of the change now I have got back to my home.

The hopes expressed in this, the last sentence of Sir Daniel Gooch's Diary, were not destined to be realised.

After many weeks of suffering, patiently borne, he died on October 15th, 1889, and was buried in Clewer Churchyard, adjoining the pleasant gardens of that home to which his thoughts had so often turned.

1. This voyage was satisfactorily accomplished.
2. Now the Earl of Bessborough.
3. Mr. Charles Gooch, Sir Daniel's second son.
4. This attempt was unsuccessful.
5. The Cornwall Railway was taken over in 1889, bringing the total mileage of the Great Western Railway up to 2536 miles.
6. The Severn Tunnel is 4 miles and 624 yards long. It is part of a line of railway which connects the Great Western Railway at Bristol with the South Wales Branch west of Chepstow.
7. General Manager of the Great Western Railway.
8. See above, page 48.

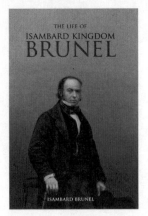
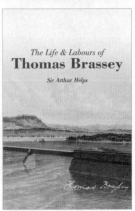
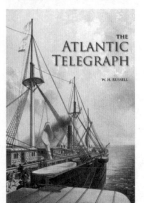